For Betsy —

THE SEVEN FACES OF
LEADERSHIP

Robert

THE SEVEN FACES OF
LEADERSHIP

ROBERT J. ALLIO

This book was printed in the United States of America.

Cover art Vasily Kandinsky, with permission of Peggy Guggenheim Museum

To order additional copies of this book, contact:
Xlibris Corporation
1-888-795-4274
www.Xlibris.com
Orders@Xlibris.com
15962-ALLI

Contents

List of Exhibits

Preface

The Seven Faces of Leadership represents an effort to formulate a grand unifying theory of leadership for those who direct our contemporary organizations. Is a leader made or born? Must leadership style be tailored to the situation? Are there universal leadership virtues? Can we teach our followers to become leaders? This book addresses these questions and many others.

Without apology, I offer the reader a serious treatise on leadership that will require some effort to absorb. This is not the 60-minute or 60-hour treatise that supplies all you need to know about leadership in one easy read. But for those willing to invest time and energy, I promise new insights into leadership and the leadership process.

The findings in my studies are based in part on the premise that we learn to be leaders by observing other leaders. Since the cohort of contemporary leaders is so impoverished, we must turn to history and literature for inspiration. Although I've drawn many of my examples of leader's failure and success from the corporate world, we can mine splendid insights on how to lead and how to become a leader not only from business journals but also from literary and philosophical veins. As an example, consider Shakespeare's stories of leaders like Hamlet (who acts too deliberately), Othello (who acts too rashly), Lear (who can't let go of his power), Henry V (who can let go of his identity as Prince Hal as the rake).

You may think it unusual that this book has mixed together

examples of leadership at times of crisis from so many periods of history, both ancient and modern. They were selected for a reason. I believe that the leadership lessons from antiquity connect us to a treasure trove of knowledge about changing culture and behavior at a decisive moment in time—in other words, how leaders accomplish transformation. These lessons from history provide guidance to leaders today in ways that the daily business pages cannot.

Who should read this book? Leaders eager to improve their performance, and those in leadership positions who want to learn how to actually become a leader. Those who have a responsibility to select leaders and develop future leaders. And those who are interested in a perspective on leadership that looks beyond the antics of many contemporary leaders.

Because there are so few examples of good leaders to study, it's much easier to identify flawed leadership. So in part, we can only arrive at our models of effective leadership by a process of elimination. The field is still open for research on a number of important aspects of the subject. We desperately need data that establish clear correlation between leadership attributes and organizational performance. We need to understand better the leadership development process, the role of diversity, the most effective approach to managing change. But *The Seven Faces of Leadership* offers a good starting point to contemplate these issues.

Acknowledgements

I thank all those who carefully reviewed and commented on early versions of the manuscript, especially Dorothy Kramer-Kawakami, Thomas Naylor, Malcolm Pennington, and Walter Schaffir. Stan Abraham and Robert Randall offered invaluable and abundant critique of some of my many facile assertions, as well as my lapses into pedantry. Albert Anderson was my touchstone for many philosophical explorations. And conversations with the practitioners of leadership (Gary Mecklenburg and Kathy Murray of Northwestern Memorial, Diego and Diegui Suarez of the V. Suárez Group, and Desi DeSimone of 3M), gave me a forum in which to test hypotheses. Michael Allio and Paul Allio provided continuing critical input; Angela Gendron and Pamela Champagne gave ongoing editorial support, and Christopher Allio supported the graphics presentations.

Chapter 1

Introduction

Challenges abound in these times of uncertainty and flux. As leaders seek opportunity and manage risk, their goal is to excel, not merely to endure. Yet after many years of studying the behavior of leaders, there is no uniformly accepted definition of leadership and what it entails.

Consider the difficulty we have in answering these crucial questions:

- Where do leaders come from?
- What are the essential tasks that all leaders must address?
- Is leadership situational, or can we identify certain leadership constants?
- Does leadership style matter?
- What are the quintessential skills that any leader must exhibit?
- Do leaders share a certain set of personal qualities?
- How can we, as aspiring leaders, compensate for our inevitable flaws?
- Can men and women be taught to become more effective leaders?
- Can any leader sustain high performance over a long period of time?
- What is the best measure of effective leadership?
- How will the role of the leader change as we move into the 21st century?

Before reading on, however, I suggest that you formulate your own response to these questions. Test and perhaps modify your responses as you consider my own conclusions in the following chapters.

Let's be clear at the outset about terminology, for the popular literature uses the terms *leader* and *leadership* in a variety of ways.[1] As a consequence, common usage often confounds organizational status (a person's rank in the hierarchy) with leadership itself. (We've all witnessed the abysmal lack of leadership behavior on the part of individuals who hold prominent positions.) Furthermore, common usage doesn't differentiate tyrants—who have authority, but demean their followers—from effective leaders—who may have little or no authority, but lead their organizations toward constructive end states.

To start, let us adopt the following simple definitions:

Leader = a man or woman who influences the beliefs and behavior of a community.
Leadership = the process or act of leading.

Good leaders repeatedly do the right thing in the right way (but not invariably—one of the hallmarks of leadership is the ability to recover from and learn from a failure or misjudgment). Leaders awaken in their followers a sense of a higher potential. Tyrants, dictators, or charlatans may enlist followers in their cause, but lead them astray. They *mis*lead their followers into dystopia, a state where conditions are morally or economically intolerable. Leaders, in other words, may be virtuous or corrupt. Virtuous leaders advance the welfare of the community. Corrupt leaders (the misleaders) retard or subvert the development of the community.

A common misconception is that leaders are heroic. Although leaders may behave heroically from time to time, heroism does not equate to leadership. A leader displays a

---

1 The term leader (mi leder) appears in the English language for the first time in about AD 1300, according to the Oxford English Dictionary.

pattern of behavior that results from a succession of leadership acts. Good leaders leave an imprint on their times and their institutions. A hero by contrast may perform only a single act of nobility or courage, sometimes at risk of his or her life, to avert disaster or achieve success, be it in war, sports or business. Thus the hero saves the child from the burning building or scores the winning touchdown. And heroes may act alone; leaders always have followers.

Nor does most management literature distinguish clearly between a manager—who is in charge of implementing a particular set of short-term tasks—and the leader, who must create an attractive future for the organization. But the classic dichotomy that management theorists have established between leading and managing is simplistic and artificial. Leaders must *manage* to achieve outcomes, and managers cannot succeed unless they also *lead*. Managers can be characterized as leaders who have restricted options because of their limited power or subordinate position in the organization. However, managers at any level in an organization can behave as leaders; they can discover opportunities and prepare their teams to excel at meeting them.

With this caveat, however, we can say that the primary challenge for leaders is to transform their organizations and maintain their viability through a continuing process of self-renewal. The primary challenge for managers is to implement and help formulate strategy and programs. Leaders are concerned with behavior that allows us to reach a desirable end state; they manage the future. Managers worry about today's tasks, or perhaps tomorrow's. Leaders inspire and motivate, while managers delegate and control. Leaders foster innovation, while managers strive to realize stability. The managerial perspective tends to be amoral—managers make decisions based on pure pragmatism, ignoring the nuances of value and higher moral purpose. Managers can treat individuals as means to an end that has already been specified.

Leaders in comparison are strongly concerned with ethical principles; they worry about both means and ends. Exhibit 1-1 summarizes the important differences.

| 1.1 | LEADING AND MANAGING ARE COMPLEMENTARY |

Leader	Manager
Takes the long view	Takes the short view
Formulates visions	Makes plans, budgets
Takes risks	Avoids risks
Explores new territory	Maintains existing patterns
Initiates change	Stabilizes
Transforms	Transacts
Empowers	Controls
Encourages diversity	Enforces uniformity
Invokes passion	Invokes rationality
Acts morally	Acts amorally

One further distinction can be drawn between leaders and managers. The manager's worldview is predominantly linear and analytic. Detailed analysis of the situation, computation of probabilities to address future ambiguity or uncertainty, assessment of resources and risks, evaluation of expected financial returns—all are standard elements in the manager's inventory of tools. When analysis has been completed, the organization assesses its choices, embraces a set of decisions (a synonym for a strategy) and proceeds with implementation. The leader's worldview gives purpose and vision to the enterprise, and his or her strategic decisions link values and vision. Exhibit 1-2 depicts the relationship between the two mindsets.

1.2 | LEADERS AND MANAGERS HAVE DIFFERENT PERSPECTIVES

Vision

Analysis ···· ·>   Strategy   ··· ·> Implementation

Values and Purpose

The archetypal leader brings other dimensions to the decision-making process. He or she complements the cool Apollonian rationality of the archetypal manager by bringing Dionysian passion to the organization, and this passion and commitment often overrides reason and rationality. Thus, the feelings and intuition of the leader—what the leader feels in his or her heart and soul is the right thing to do—augment the detached rationality of the manager. Those who exalt rationality are handicapped by their adherence to a fixed business model, one based on linear extrapolation from the present, or more often the past. *How we choose* to act, the leader will argue, may be more important than *what we choose* to do, although good leaders must pay attention to both.[2] Passion untempered by reason may yield folly. But reason uninformed by passion will never inspire.

Leaders do falter when they step over the line between passionate commitment to a great vision and obsessive monomania or extreme ambition. Consider these cases:

2 Existentialists Søren Kierkegaard and Jean-Paul Sartre are well-known advocates of passionate commitment, and novelist Fyodor Dostoevsky charges that enslavement to rationality is not better than enslavement to passion. British philosopher David Hume exhorts man to use reason as the servant of passion.

- Ken Olsen was a brilliant engineer who capitalized on IBM's inertia in developing the minicomputer to create the Digital Equipment Corporation. But Olsen himself refused to adapt to new technology and customer needs. By the time his board of directors ousted him, it was too late. Digital continued to lose ground and in the end was acquired by Compaq Computer. By contrast, Steve Jobs returned to Apple Computer after his ouster and strengthened Apple's position in the personal computer market through new products and technology.

- John DeLorean, former General Motors executive, attempted to develop a new market niche for the automobile by introducing an innovative aluminum car. But DeLorean seemed to ignore all the other key success factors in the industry—distribution, quality, and cost. His company struggled for a few years and then plunged into bankruptcy. Lee Iacocca, by contrast, helped by a major infusion of cash from the Federal Government, was able to bring Chrysler back from the brink of bankruptcy.

- Donald Burnham founded People Express in an inspired effort to serve the frequent flyer in the Boston-to-New York-to-Washington corridor. But in his fervor to build teamwork and team spirit, he failed to address the fundamental economics of airline transportation, and People Express failed. Herb Kelleher, in comparison, adopted a similar customer-friendly philosophy, but made Southwest Airlines the most profitable company in the airline industry.

Any organization will benefit from an integrated, systemic, and creative approach to making decisions. Leaders will find that they achieve the best outcomes when intuition and rationality augment one another.[3] From another perspective, leading and managing represent the relative accent on effectiveness (doing the right thing) and efficiency (doing things right), between clear purpose and well-defined processes. Purpose without process leads to frustration. Efficient process without purpose engenders disengagement: a total bureaucracy may ensue.[4] Energized organizations score high on both dimensions. Many of the more that 300 Internet businesses launched in the 1998-99 period are egregious examples of enterprises that lacked both process and purpose—and most have crashed and burned.

When to lead? When to manage? Herman Melville presents the manager/leader dilemma in his story of *Billy Budd*. John Claggart, the unscrupulous Master of Arms, falsely accuses Billy, a sailor on Captain Vere's British warship, of treason. Billy strikes and kills his accuser. Although Vere loves Billy as a son, he decides to uphold the law and hang Billy for his capital offense. Vere's primary obligation, he reasons, is to preserve social order: justice surpasses mercy as a criterion for his decision. Billy appears to understand, crying out "God bless Captain Vere," just before he is hanged. In his role as a manager, Vere follows the rules—he is bound to do his duty. As a leader, however, he has an opportunity to make a decision that reflects the mitigating circumstances of Billy's crime. Good leaders invoke compassion and mercy in establishing criteria for decisions (see Chapter 9).

Leaders must respond to exactly these kinds of challenge to creativity. Vere, like all leaders, needs to do more than

---

3 This complementarity is the analog of Danish physicist Nils Bohr's reconciliation of the behavior of light as both a particle and a wave. We can view light in either way, but not both ways at once. Yet both concepts are necessary to describe reality.

4 Franz Kafka's protagonist in his 1926 novel *The Castle* is our literary analog. Indicted for an unknown crime, K, the land surveyor, must wend his way through a bureaucratic maze in search of explanation.

follow old rules. He needs to understand the reality of Billy's situation and balance justice with mercy.[5]

To recapitulate, then, we find that effective heads of organizations balance their time and energy between leading and managing. Over-leading and under-managing is just as bad as under-leading and over-managing. Practical leaders learn to delegate many managerial tasks. And in the long run, leaders must also be prepared to delegate or share the leadership role.

When did all this attention to the nuances of leadership start? The leadership paradigm has intrigued man at least since the introduction of the Tarot, a deck of divination cards developed in ancient Egypt. The Tarot presents several leadership types in the Major Arcana, which comprise 21 of the 78 cards. These include both religious leaders (the Hierophant and the High Priestess) and political leaders (the Emperor and the Empress). Joseph Campbell, the noted anthropologist and cultural historian, has documented the leadership stereotype found in the mythologies of cultures around the world.[6]

We can learn a great deal about leadership from the many case histories found in world literature. In his *Iliad* and *Odyssey*, written in the 8th century BC, Homer documents the saga of Ulysses leading his men through a series of major challenges before reaching home. Plutarch, the 1st century Greek historian and philosopher, writes at length in *Plutarch's Lives* about the leaders of ancient Rome. Shakespeare, writing for us in the 16th century, catalogues at length the follies and triumphs of Lear, Macbeth, Hamlet, Richard III, Henry V, and other kings and princes. Machiavelli, the 15th century Italian political theorist, is remembered primarily for his advice to leaders on how to rule.

---

5 Leaders on the battlefield, of course, need to maintain a high degree of control and discipline. In a corporation, on the other hand, employees can simply quit and join the competition.

6 See, for example, his *The Hero with a Thousand Faces*, Princeton University Press, 1968.

All of these writers illustrate or prescribe leadership behavior rather than explicating it. Nevertheless, their case histories have more to offer than much of the explanatory literature on leadership and leaders that historians, political scientists, psychologists, and management theorists have produced since the mid-20th century.

If you seek a book on the subject today, Amazon.com lists an impressive 1836 choices for leader and 9818 for leadership. The Google (www.google.com) and Northern Lights (www.northernlights.com) search engines disgorge literally millions of references to leaders and leadership. Despite this expository torrent, the countless biographies of leaders from Jesus Christ and Attila the Hun to Jack Welch, former chairman of General Electric (GE), the innumerable empirical studies of leadership, we lack a Grand Unifying Theory that definitively identifies the source code or essence of leaders and defines the conditions that produce leaders.

The obstacles to arriving at a clear algorithm for leadership and how to practice it include the unthinking acceptance of a number of myths. These are some of the most common:

■ Leaders are born

All potential leaders are born with certain qualities. But they develop into leaders only by forging their craft in the fire of challenge and competition.[7]

■ Leaders are heroic

Heroic leadership is short-lived. And it becomes unnecessary if the leader succeeds in building community and raising its collective performance. As the Native Americans observe with insight, one finger cannot lift a pebble.

---

7 William Shakespeare's catch-all summary: "some are born great, some achieve greatness, and some have greatness thrust upon them," *Twelfth Night*, Act II.

- Leaders maintain stability in the organization

Stability is the precursor to atrophy. Leaders initiate the changes that permit the organization to adapt to inevitable challenges from the environment and to evolve to a higher state.

- Leaders can be taught

Leadership cannot be taught by exposure to convenient academic modules, despite the allegations of many leadership gurus. Paradoxically, however, men and women can learn to be leaders by developing a set of core leadership skills and qualities—by teaching themselves. Leadership potential is activated by practice.

- Leadership is measured best by today's results, such as quarterly profits

Short-term results—conquests or victories—may not contribute to long-term prosperity or welfare.[8] Both by what they do and how they act, leaders make an enduring imprint on their organizations. The ultimate measure of a leader's greatness is his or her legacy.

Before we continue, let's address society's current obsession with leadership. Some skeptical European writers have explained the interest in the subject as either another peculiarly American fad or organizational cultism. The French, for example, have no equivalent term, using *le leadership* when discussing the topic. The Italians have stigmatized the term *il duce*, relating it to the negative outcome of Mussolini's regime during World W107ar II. The Germans assign sinister implications to *Führershaft*, a word associated with Adolf Hitler's regime. But Europeans embraced the monarchist system of rule for centuries—

---

8 George Washington lost almost every battle he fought, but he still won the war for U.S. independence.

except for the brief reign of George III, the U.S. colonists never had a king or queen!

Nevertheless, in our experience as managers or executives we can all recall that the first order of business for a new group is usually to select a leader. This may be a reflection of our own lack of confidence in the task to be undertaken. Or our need in times of uncertainty to find a charismatic father figure in whom to place our trust. But in my view, it most often results from our collective experience that groups having a leader are more effective than those who lack one.

Power and authority may be distributed or may shift from person to person or from group to group. But leadership is still the prerequisite for high performance. Effective leaders make a difference—they produce good results over a sustained period of time. Looking back in time, we can see that many great undertakings might have been abandoned without the galvanizing force of leadership. The bold enterprises, the large complex projects of our civilization, did not materialize without a leader who motivated a community of individuals to achieve their vision. Consider some of the following examples.

The Great Pyramid of Egypt, the first (and only survivor) of the Seven Wonders of the Ancient World, was conceived and directed by King Khufu during his reign from 2551 to 2528 B.C. He assembled two crews of 2000 workers and a support staff of over 25,000 to complete the project. The Manhattan Project, initiated during the Second World War to harness the power of the atom, owes its success to the inspiration and leadership of physicist J. Robert Oppenheimer. NASA's Apollo Project, which finally succeeded in placing a man on the moon for the first time in 1969, was the result of President John F. Kennedy's inspiration and the leadership of the NASA team. In the corporate world, the great firms of our era—Ford, General Electric, General Motors, Intel, 3M, Microsoft, Wal-Mart and others, all benefited from leaders who set the stage for continuing growth and high performance.

We start, then, with the premise that effective leadership is the precursor to high performance in any organization. We've all seen examples of poor leadership—and many of us have endured the burden of mediocre leadership. But what about good leadership—what must a good leader do to serve his or her constituents effectively? He or she builds an organization on three pillars:

- Explicit values and a clear sense of purpose

The effective leader affirms the meaning and purpose of the work that the organization carries out. Archetypes of value-driven leadership include James Burke, former Chairman of Johnson & Johnson, the diversified health-care corporation, and Aaron Feuerstein, Chairman of textile manufacturer Malden Mills.

- Vision and strategic direction

Good leaders envision the goals and objectives of the organization and help the organization define the strategy to get there. As the environment changes, the organization must adapt, and it must continually refine and sometimes reinvent completely its vision. And the rapid change that we're all experiencing demands that our leaders have even greater vision than before!

Archetypal vision-driven organizations include Microsoft, led by Chairman Bill Gates, Intel, formerly led by Chairman Andrew Grove, and Amazon.com, founded by CEO Jeff Bezos.

- A community that has the resources and will to implement the strategy

The success of any leader ultimately hinges on his or her ability to forge a group of individuals who will work together to realize their individual and collective potential. Without committed and effective followers working toward an appropriate goal, the leader who recognizes the need to prepare for a coming crisis is no more than a street-corner Cassandra.[9] The importance of community increases as the historic loyalty of employees to their firms diminishes, driven in part by the frequent and abrupt downsizings we're witnessing in many industries.

Archetypes of community-driven firms include Southwest Airlines (led by CEO Herb Kelleher) and Wal-Mart (founded by Sam Walton).

Building and maintaining these three complementary pillars constitutes the overarching agenda for any leader. In the next several chapters, we'll elaborate on the role of the leader in meeting the demands of this agenda. We'll demonstrate that all leaders govern with an appropriate style, they exhibit certain skills, they exhibit certain qualities, including the will to lead, and they seize the opportunity to serve as leaders.

It will become clear that leaders are multidimensional— they have seven faces and responsibilities. To be a leader is to fill a set of roles, each of which satisfies a critical organizational need and objective. The *purposeful leader* addresses values and purpose. The *visionary leader* focuses on the future of the enterprise. The *strategic leader* develops the action plan necessary to realize the vision. The *beneficent leader* attends to the needs of the community. The *adaptive leader* helps the organization respond to the new demands of the environment. The *guiding leader* prepares followers to carry on the traditions of the organization. The *virtuous leader* practices the qualities required to be effective. All of these persona represent the faces of an effective leader and

---

9 In Greek mythology, the god Apollo granted Cassandra the gift of prophecy. When she refused to return his love, he decreed that no one would believe her predictions.

constitute an agenda that any aspiring leader must adopt. (Exhibit 1-3)

| 1.3 | THE 7 FACES OF LEADERSHIP |

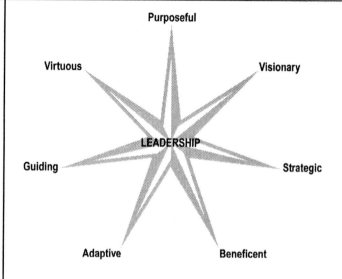

Take the diagnostic (Exhibit 1-4) to assess your own beliefs about leadership. Then continue with Chapter 2, as we review some of the existing theories of leadership and the leadership process.

1.4 | LEADERSHIP DIAGNOSTIC

Values and Purpose

+ We have published a formal statement of values
+ Values are invoked in important decisions
+ We review the value statement each year for clarity and relevance
+ We teach our values to new employees

Vision

+ We have explored alternative future scenarios
+ Our vision statement describes the desired future for the organization
+ The vision has a time horizon of more than 3 years
+ Many in the organization contributed to formulate the vision

Strategy

+ We have a formal strategic plan
+ The strategy links values and vision
+ The plan has been widely distributed
+ Managers allocate resources according to the plan
+ Performances measures are explicit
+ The reward system recognizes strategy implementation

Community

+ The culture of the firm is easy to describe
+ We have adopted unique rituals and symbols
+ Our behavior is consistant with values and strategies
+ We encourage diversity and constructive dissent
+ We support risk taking and tolerate mistakes
+ Loyalty is an important corporate value

Chapter 2

Early Models of Leadership

Our goal in this chapter is to review the historic theories that have attempted to account for leadership success and failure.

Where do leaders come from?

Be the leaders men or women, we judge them by whether or not they make a difference. Leo Tolstoy had a contrary view. In *War and Peace*, he asserts with assurance that "A king is history's slave." [1] Why does an apple fall, he asks. Gravity, the wind, decay? Nothing (and everything) is the cause, he concludes, and he goes on to dispel the myth of Napoleon as a great leader. Tolstoy claims that so-called acts of great leadership, such as Napoleon's invasion of Russia, were only the culmination of an entire series of prior events, each dependent on one another. Napoleon could not have been individually responsible for commanding the invasion and never did so; the event occurred because of the collective activity of many people.

Georg Wilhelm Friedrich Hegel's historic determinism echoes Tolstoy.[2] According to Hegel, history simply unfolds. The leader is the pawn in a script that has been prewritten, and therefore leadership is a mirage. Even Richard Nixon

---

1 Leo Tolstoy, *War and Peace*, The Heritage Press, 1938.
2 Georg Wilhelm Friedrich Hegel, *Lectures on the Philosophy of History*, J. Sibree, 1956.

admitted that "I don't think that a leader can control to any great extent his destiny. Very seldom can he step in and change the situation if the forces of history are running in another direction."[3] Nixon's view, of course, reflects the constraints experienced by most political leaders, who have few degrees of freedom within which to act.

In a position diametrically opposed to Tolstoy and Hegel, however, the Scottish historian Thomas Carlyle proclaims in 1841 that "The history of what man has accomplished in this world is at bottom the History of the Great Men who have worked here."[4] According to this argument, it is the individual leader who is responsible for the great events or periods in the history of a civilization or an organization.

The evidence does not support fully either the fortuitous or heroic models of leadership. I postulate that Napoleon distinguished himself *precisely because* he was able to develop the collective support of committed followers. Other heroic leaders, such as Carlyle's Great Men, would not have succeeded without similar support; in the long run, a leader who individually attempts to alter the course of history will fail.

The emergence of leadership in any case depends upon the circumstances of the times. When an organization is static or when the environment is placid, true leadership rarely arises. In such unconfused times, caretakers can maintain the status quo. Tolstoy speaks with special eloquence, however, about the failure of these leaders in turbulent times:

In quiet and untroubled times it seems to every administrator that it is only by his efforts that the whole population under his rule is kept going, and in this consciousness of being indispensable every administrator finds the chief reward of his labor and efforts. When the sea of history remains calm, the ruler-administrator in his frail

---

3 Richard M. Nixon, quoted in Earl Mazo's *Richard Nixon, A Political and Personal Portrait*, Harper, 1959.

4 Thomas Carlyle, *On Heroes, Hero-Worship, and the Heroic in History*, University of California Press, 1993.

bark, holding on with a boat hook to the ship of the people and himself moving, naturally imagines that his efforts move the ship he is holding onto. But as soon as a storm arises and the sea begins to heave and the ship to move, such a delusion is no longer possible. The ship moves independently with its own enormous motion, the boat hook no longer reaches the moving vessel, and suddenly the administrator, instead of appearing a ruler and source of power, becomes an insignificant, useless feeble man.

Thus, when a challenge to the welfare of the state or the group occurs, leadership has its moment to prove itself. Indeed, many individuals who possess the requisite qualities and skills will remain dormant leaders until they are challenged to respond to a crisis. (Would we revere Lincoln's leadership if history had not offered him the challenge of freeing the slaves and preserving the Union? Will we continue to admire George W. Bush as he deals with the challenge of sudden economic deficits, terrorist threats, the Enron scandals?)

The inequities confronted by the African-Americans in the U.S. brought Martin Luther King, Jr. to prominence as the leader of the civil rights movement in the 1960s; and the discrimination against the blacks in South Africa as a result of apartheid brought Nelson Mandela to power in the 1980s. Mandela was eventually elected the first black President of South Africa. Oppression by the Polish government in 1980 inspired Lech Walesa, a labor union official, to organize workers at the Gdansk shipyard to strike in reaction. The workers' initiatives led to the formation of the national solidarity movement. Walesa was awarded the Nobel Peace Prize in 1983 and was elected president of Poland in 1990.

In business organizations, economic conditions usually precipitate the crisis: a decline in revenues, profit, or cash flow. Of course, even a crisis may not arouse leadership potential—as note Herbert Hoover's failure to deal with the Great Depression of the 1930s. Conversely, a potential leader may simply bring a new vision or search for excellence to the organization—or may be driven to form a new enterprise to achieve a particular personal vision, as in the case of many entrepreneurs. Indeed, great leaders may not only respond to a crisis first but actually create crisis as they endeavor to achieve a bold new vision.

Among the leaders of large corporations, Ted Turner of CNN and Bill Gates of Microsoft fall into this category. The religious domain offers us many examples of messianic visionaries—the Buddha, Jesus Christ, Muhammad, Joseph Smith (founder of the Church of Jesus Christ of Latter Day Saints), and Mary Baker Eddy (founder of the Church of Christ, Scientist).

In times of peace and prosperity, the majority see no need for the sacrifices that strong leaders may demand of them. When chaos develops, however, stakeholders seek order and inspiration, and they are prepared to accept a savior who can lead them through the trials of the desert and eventually out of the wilderness, a strong leader like Winston Churchill or Franklin Delano Roosevelt who can provide a sense of security.

Unfortunately, this state of mind may foster the emergence of charismatic leaders with dependent followers who exhibit a "devotion born of distress." The interaction in this situation between leaders and followers often creates a destructive pathology, and, in the absence of strong moral leadership, the organization may devolve into a cult, as was the case with Jim Jones at Jonestown.

In 1978, Jones, a former San Francisco clergyman, established a commune in Jonestown, Guyana. After U.S. congressman Leo Ryan arrived to investigate complaints that some of his constituents' relatives were being mistreated, Jones had 914 of his followers commit suicide by drinking Kool-Aid spiked with cyanide. Jones later shot himself, and Ryan was killed by Jones' loyalists.

A similar tragedy occurred in 1993 in Waco, Texas. David

Koresh, the leader of the Branch Davidian fundamentalist cult, stockpiled an arsenal near Waco. When the FBI moved in to investigate, cult members set fire to the arsenal, killing more than 80 of their members, including children.[5]

Are leaders made or born? The evidence suggests that leadership emerges when individuals seize an opportunity to develop themselves as leaders. They become leaders when they are given the chance to *practice* the craft of leadership in a challenging situation. They may fail (John Akers at IBM), succeed (Lee Iacocca at Chrysler), or exploit the opportunity to mislead (Albert Dunlap at Sunbeam).

Models for leadership success and failure

How do we explain the success or failure of men and women who assume leadership roles? The theorists of the early twentieth century were convinced that leadership was the consequence of an individual's traits, qualities, or intrinsic attributes. In this simplest of explanatory models, traits produce the leader. Most writers abandoned these trait theories, after it became clear that leaders exhibit a wide range of qualities. Furthermore, while a particular set of qualities may be necessary to support the leading of an organization, it alone will not ensure success. But even today, writers are fond of compiling lists of virtues held in common by leaders—persistence, passion, conviction, integrity, courage, trust, curiosity, daring.

The evidence does support the idea that exceptional leaders share certain qualities, including a strong personal ethic and set of values, coupled with a compelling vision of the future. Extensive research, however, has failed to uncover

---

5 Several federal agents were killed in an earlier attempt to arrest cult members who were stockpiling automatic weapons.
6 Ralph Stodgill, among others, reaches this conclusion after reviewing 120 studies of leadership. "Personal Factors Associated with Leadership," Journal of Psychology, 25, 1948.

any statistically significant correlation between a leader's effectiveness and his personal characteristics.[6] Some writers suggest, in fact, that followers simply attribute certain qualities to a leader, based on their own perceptions. Charismatic leadership is another variant of this model.

An early form of trait theory was the generational succession practiced by the monarchies of Europe. In an exercise of primogeniture, Kings or Queens simply passed the leadership mantle to the first-born child, presumably the child best-equipped (by divine right) to defend the realm.

A similar succession model figures prominently in the planning of many contemporary corporations. Boards of directors often select new leaders from the next in line, typically the man (less often the woman) who has accumulated the greatest seniority. As a result, organizations, while not the victims of genetic inbreeding (except in some family firms) lose vitality because the new leader is a product of the old culture. Such a person often bears remarkable physical and psychological similarity to his or her predecessor. The resulting perpetuation of old views leads inevitably to ossification and decrepitude. After all, over a century ago, Charles Darwin showed genetic diversity to be essential to survival. In a pool of individuals exhibiting diverse characteristics, it is the fittest who survive. Even small mutations in functional capability may allow a species to adapt more readily to new challenges from the environment.

Attempts to correlate leadership and psychological type have proved no more successful than the claims of astrologers that those born under certain signs (like Leos) are "natural leaders." The most extensive analyses of type have utilized the Myers-Briggs Type Indicator (MBTI), a psychological instrument based on Carl Jung's theory of types. (The Consulting Psychologists Press claims that over three million individuals used their version of the instrument in 2001.) MBTI theorists tell us that behavior can be explained by differences in how people

- Focus their attention—extraversion (E) or introversion (I)

The Importance of Birth Order

Harvard scholar Frank Sulloway's recent research explores the significance of birth order in determining the personality and social outlook of leaders.[7] First-borns, according to Sulloway, have a conformist mindset; as conservatives, they support the status quo. Most political leaders, including U.S. Presidents and British prime ministers, are first-borns. But many leaders show the classic traits of later-borns, who take more risks and tend to be the radical innovators. They often become the iconoclasts of our society. Joan of Arc, Martin Luther, Karl Marx, and Vladimir Lenin are examples of later-borns. In the corporate world, we find leadership represented by both first-borns and later-borns. First-borns include Alfred Sloan (General Motors), Ted Turner (CNN), Jack Welch (GE), and Thomas J. Watson (IBM); later-borns include Lee Iacocca (Chrysler), Walter Wriston (Citicorp), and Ross Perot (EDS). The evidence demonstrates, then, that birth order is at best a second-order influence on leadership.

- Take in information—by sensing (S) or intuiting (N)
- Make decisions—by thinking (T) or feeling (F)
- Relate to the outside world—by judging (J) or perceiving (P)

The combination of these preferences produces 16 personality types. Studies show that thinking and judging dominate across both culture and organization type. Women, 65% of whom exhibit feeling preference in the general

---

7 Frank J. Sulloway, *Born to Rebel*, Pantheon, 1996.

population, shift to thinking preference when they join management ranks. When managers shift to roles as leaders, we can infer that it may be important to shift from an ST/SJ type to a NF/NP type who can develop vision and arouse excitement in the organization. However, research has never generated data linking MBTI personality type with leadership effectiveness. Although Isabel Briggs, one of the architects of the system, refers to ENTJ types as "leaders of leaders," we can find ample evidence of leadership in each of the 16 types.

The Myers-Briggs system lacks the specificity and depth to illuminate the function of leadership (it fails to help us in a quest for new leaders, for example). A more useful personality system is based on the Enneagram. Developed originally by the Sufis, the Enneagram was introduced to the West by the Russian mystic Georges Gurdjieff in 1916, Chilean spiritual teacher Oscar Ichazo in 1970, and U.S. psychiatrist Claudio Naranjo in the 1970s.[8] The Enneagram identifies nine basic personality types, each deriving from a fundamental perceptual filter that influences where we place our attention, and hence our energy. Exhibit 2-1 summarizes the nine types and their leadership strengths and challenges. Types 1, 3, and 8, according to Enneagram theory, tend to lead directly; other types, like 5, may prefer to lead indirectly.

Because early trait theories lacked explanatory power, however, by the 1950s theories based on leadership style became popular. These new models proposed that style—how the leader interacted with the followers—was the primary determinant of leadership effectiveness. The most famous of these models was Douglas McGregor's useful concept of Theory X and Theory Y, which contrasted the merits of autocratic style (Theory X) with participative style (Theory Y).[9]

8 Helen Palmer has taken the lead recently in promoting the use of the Enneagram. See, for example, *The Enneagram Advantage*, Three Rivers Press, 1997.
9 Douglas McGregor, *The Human Side of Enterprise*, McGraw-Hill, 1960.

Subsequent analysts suggested a two-dimensional map that portrayed the relative importance of task orientation and relationship to subordinates.

The Blake-Mouton grid, as one example, served as the foundation module in many management development programs, although the theory originally emphasized management style as opposed to leadership competence.[10] This model assigned a scale of 1 to 9 to each of two coordinates: concern for task and concern for relationships. Team leaders give equally strong attention to the task and to relationships, resulting in a score of (9,9). Authoritarian managers adopt (9,1) orientations, which stress getting the job done. "Country-club" managers have (1,9) orientations, which place priority on good interpersonal relationships. Although Blake later augmented his grid by adding a third dimension to account for motivation (or lack of motivation) as an important variable in determining performance, it has limited application to explaining leadership. It does merit our attention, however, as a precursor to the current fad of "emotional intelligence."

Behavioral models based on style have the virtue of simplicity, but the correlation between performance and leadership style alone has always been weak. As a consequence, leadership scholars turned to contingency models. These models hypothesize that leadership effectiveness is the result of the interaction among three variables: the nature of the task (what has to get done), the relationship between leaders and followers, and the power inherent in the leader and his or her position.

The most comprehensive of the contingency models adds another variable: the readiness of the followers to perform.[11] When followers are able and willing, leaders can delegate responsibility for decisions and their implementation. Able

10 Robert R. Blake and Jane S. Mouton, *The Managerial Grid*, 1964.
11 Paul Hersey, *Situational Leadership*, Center for Creative Leadership, 1995.
12 James MacGregor Burns, *Leadership*, Harper & Row, 1978.

but unwilling or insecure followers require a participative style of leadership. Willing but unskilled followers need instruction, and unable or unwilling followers need both instruction and close supervision.

The contingency models may reassure potential leaders who are seeking a rationale for their own approach to leadership—anything may work, in other words. And these models do have a commonsensical appeal (when the building is burning, let's not sit around and discuss what to do!) But they fail to give us an algorithm for effective leadership that embraces all the key variables.

The shortcomings of contingency models were underscored in the 1990s when political scientist James MacGregor Burns introduced the useful distinction between transforming leaders and transactional leaders.[12] Transactions describe the normal interaction between leaders and followers— the transactional leader offers rewards in exchange for the performance of certain tasks. Transforming leaders, on the other hand, satisfy the higher needs of the followers. They interact with followers to raise the organization to a higher moral plane. Burns' examples of transforming leaders, drawn primarily from the political domain, include Simon Bolivar, Fidel Castro, and Ho Chi Minh.

Some other recent expositions of leadership fall into the category of Aristotle's virtue theory: leaders are those who do the right thing—they do good works. Author James O'Toole, for example, contrasts the pragmatism of GE's Jack Welch—who adopts corporate policies because they work— with the morality of Max DePree, former CEO of furniture manufacturer Herman Miller—who adopts corporate policies because they are right.[13] Joseph Badaracco advocates

13 Max DePree, *Leadership is an Art*, Dell, 1989.
14 Joseph L. Badarocco, Jr., *Leading Quietly*, Harvard Business School Press, 2002.
15 Daniel Goleman, Richard Boyatzis, Annie McKee, *Primal Leadership*, Harvard Business School Press, 2002.

"leading quietly"—choosing responsible behind-the-scenes action over public heroism to resolve tough leadership challenges.[14] And "primal leadership" is proposed by the advocates of emotional intelligence as the key to effectiveness.[15]

Harvard psychologist Howard Gardner distinguishes between ordinary leaders, innovative leaders, and visionary leaders.[16] According to his model, ordinary leaders (former U.S. President Gerald Ford, former General Motors Chairman Roger Smith) tell the same old stories. Innovative leaders (French President Charles de Gaulle, British Prime Minister Margaret Thatcher, perhaps U.S. President Ronald Reagan) take a latent story and retell it with creativity. The visionary leaders, like Jesus, Moses, the Buddha, and Gandhi create entirely new stories.

None of these models, unfortunately, is complete, and none offers much more than fragmentary guidance on how to improve our leadership skills and effectiveness. We need a better road map, a more robust and comprehensive model. In the following chapters we will provide some new perspectives on

> ➤ The four central tasks of a leader
> ➤ The best leadership style
> ➤ The critical skills that a leader must cultivate
> ➤ The essential leadership qualities
> ➤ The best metric for evaluating leadership effectiveness

These elements collectively will constitute the seven faces of leadership. In the next chapter, we'll begin by examining the nature of the *purposeful leader.*

---

16 Howard Gardner, *Leading Minds*, Basic Books, 1995. In his recent discussion of extraordinary individuals, Gardner differentiates between masters (Wolfgang Amadeus Mozart), makers (Sigmund Freud), introspectors (Virginia Woolf), and influencers (Mahatma Gandhi).

Exhibit 2.1
The Enneagram Leadership Matrix

LEADERSHIP STYLE	CLARIFY VALUES	SET DIRECTION	BUILD COMMUNITY	MANAGE CHANGE
One: Perfectionist Motivated to educate, reform, do the right thing; meet high internal standards; strives for continual improvement; responsible, fair and trustworthy; acts with integrity, postpones pleasure until work is done; creates and requires order and rules; may become overly-focused on eliminating mistakes.	Promotes reliability, integrity and cheerful hard work in service of a higher purpose. Emphasizes obedience to correct or moral principles and rules. Typifies philosophy of error-free performance and zero product defects.	Able to articulate the ideal version of any undertaking. The "right" direction results from rigorous and methodical adherence to clearly-stated purpose and meticulously-crafted plans, systems and procedures.	Creates a formal culture characterized by established procedures, codes of behavior and standards of excellence: employees are encouraged to act with integrity and to view hard work as a contribution to a "righteous cause."	Most comfortable in an organization where the growth path is clearly defined or in a stable environment where the rules are known. One's over-reliance on structure and procedure may exhibit an effective response to rapid changes of direction in a volatile market.
Two: Giver Motivated to meet the needs of others; creates power base through indispensability; generates good feelings among colleagues; minimizes interpersonal conflict; may be more concerned with relationships than corporate strategy; can seek attention if service not recognized.	Promotes leadership as a form of service to customers and employees. Customer satisfaction becomes primary purpose of the organization. Emphasizes the importance of communications and innovative HR policies.	Vision is informed by Two's drive to keep customers and employees satisfied. People are ultimately more important than the product or the market. Often sets direction by influencing the decisions of powerful others in the organization.	Creates a warm, humanistic culture based on mutual appreciation and support where the success, happiness and professional development of the employees is of paramount concern.	Protects customers and employees from negative impact of volatility. Creates opportunities for employees to express concerns. Two's emphasis on people issues may interfere with the making of difficult decisions.
Three: Performer Motivated to accomplish tasks and goals as a way of connecting with others and gaining their approval; confident, competent and efficient; pragmatic, adaptable; prefers tangible reward for work; crafts an image to support achievements; may allow tactics to take the place of strategy; has difficulty stopping for relaxation or self-reflection.	Promotes practical solutions to complex problems. Emphasizes the importance of speed and efficiency. Believes it is more important to succeed than to follow the rules. Perfection means "good enough to get the job done well."	Vision reflects focus on market-responsive, bottom-line, cost-effective accomplishment. The preferred direction for Threes is the most efficient road to success. Goals are clear, responsibilities are unambiguous and accountability is impartially enforced.	Creates a cheerfully-impersonal, fast-paced culture of confident, energetic single contributors who come together for the purpose of accomplishing a specific task in record time, then reform and reassemble to meet and conquer the next challenge.	Adaptability and agility enable rapid changes of direction in a volatile environment. Plans are readjusted to the new circumstances and energies are refocused on the new goal. Disruptive impact of change on non-Three employees often overlooked.
Four: Aesthetic Idealist Motivated to find deep meaning and emotional satisfaction in personal and professional life; inspires others to develop their highest potential; is creative, artistic, individualistic, and empathetic; often provides solution to every-day problems; may be overwhelmed by own emotional volatility; lose enthusiasm for tasks that lack authenticity.	Promotes authenticity of thought, action and emotional expression. Believes that it is more important to remain true to a personal vision than to compromise on someone else's game plan. Emphasizes the importance of individuality and ultimate ideals.	Vision expresses Four's passionate, often avant-garde approach. Emphasis on aesthetic presentation and intensity of experience. This "unique" direction results in extraordinary products and services developed for a discriminating clientele.	Creates an emotionally-diverse, highly-individualistic culture where originality of experience is more important than the bottom line, and where employees are encouraged to explore their inner landscape and express their true nature.	Familiarity with emotional intensity allows Four to remain committed, and even energized, during volatile times. Creativity peaks when there are tough problems to solve and significant actions to be taken. But interest and involvement may wane when work return to more normal and mundane.
Five: Observer Motivated to understand and absorb all available information on a topic; thoughtful, perceptive, and self-sufficient; protective of privacy; even in open-office environments; calm and rational in a crisis, reacts emotionally after the fact; may become overly analytical; detaching from emotions may isolate others.	Promotes personal and organizational independence and freedom of intellectual pursuit, ideas and detachment; preferred over emotional engagement. Rewards dispassionate decision making and rational responses to organizational challenges.	Vision evolves from Five's belief that relying on ideas, data and research is the way to success. Direction is the end product of meticulous, objective analysis of market realities, customer requirements and appropriate technical solutions.	Creates a culture of personal privacy and objectivity where technology is relied upon to disseminate corporate information, and where an individual's ability to accumulate and analyze information is prized over process and procedure.	As long as information remains reliable, Five's natural detachment supports an ability to implement effective responses to a volatile environment. But when intellectually taken off guard by the unexpected, Five's dislike of spontaneity may result in withdrawal of energy from the change process.

LEADERSHIP STYLE	CLARIFY VALUES	SET DIRECTION	BUILD COMMUNITY	MANAGE CHANGE
Six: Loyal Skeptic Motivated to anticipate problems and provide solutions in advance; either faces hazards directly or develops strategies to avoid them; cautious and well-prepared; inquiring mind produces imaginative ideas; loyal to cause, project or group; may doubt personal power and excellence; may magnify worst-case scenarios, put too much energy into preparing for unlikely outcomes.	Promotes loyalty to and from the organization, but will rally employees to resist abuse of authority. Emphasizes caution and foresight. Rewards willingness to present bad news with good. Believes you must do what you say and say what you mean.	Six promotes a vision that is the product of a thorough, trouble-shooter's analysis of potential pitfalls and unexpected hazards. Direction is set in response to a clearheaded, logical assessment of what it will take to manage what lies ahead.	Creates a cautious, loyal, reflective culture where information is used as a vehicle to expose and defuse hidden agendas, and where authority is held accountable to high standards of congruity between word and deed.	Six's wealth of information on meeting unforeseen challenges comes in handy when change actually occurs, and the insightful, imaginative solutions can be implemented. But if the rationale behind the need for change is not made clear, Effectiveness may be limited by self-doubt and mistrust of authority.
Seven: Positive Planner Motivated to consider multiple possibilities and interests; optimistic and future oriented; avoids conflict and unpleasantness by keeping life light; enjoys planning as much as or even more than actual accomplishment; abundant mental and physical energy; charming and egalitarian; may be diverted from the goal by a more interesting idea; chafes at limits placed on personal options.	Promotes optimism, flexibility and possibility thinking as a way to keep creativity flowing and maintain the health of the organization. Emphasizes equality of participation and responsibility. Maintains open-door policies and encourages informal communication.	Vision flows naturally from Seven's habitual, synergistic exploration of multiple creative possibilities. Direction is set and kept in motion by inspiration, enthusiasm, and willingness to risk an experiment with new products, processes and markets.	Creates an exciting, upbeat, informal, even irreverent culture that minimizes positional authority and decentralizes hierarchy in favor of a network of interdisciplinary teams focused on a revolving series of creative projects and innovative ideas.	Fascination with variety and complexity draws Seven to volatile situations and emerging markets, where the tendency to generate multiple options is a natural fit. But when things begin to stabilize, Seven may become restless, and look for opportunities to disturb the status quo and open up new possibilities.
Eight: Powerful Protector Motivated to take control of self and environment; uses big, zestful energy to assert power and promote personal truth; comfortable with confrontation; uses direct, no-frills style of communication; generous with time and personal resources; attuned to justice and protection of the less powerful; may deny personal vulnerability; may take an all-or-nothing approach that overwhelms opposition.	Promotes justice and fairness. Emphasizes truth-telling, plain speaking and open confrontation at the expense of diplomacy. Prizes gut-level decision-making over intellectual analysis. Believes that life is to be lived with gusto and total openness to experience.	Vision mirrors Eight's no-nonsense style, strong will, and entrepreneurial orientation. Direction is set by identifying a tough challenge and forcefully mobilizing the organization toward success by ignoring or eliminating internal and external obstacles.	Creates an exhilarating, risk-seeking, unusually-resilient, tough-minded culture that meets and overcomes personal and professional challenges with strength and tenacity, and is fiercely dedicated to protecting the less-powerful from organizational abuse.	Eight thrives in a rapidly-changing, demanding environment that needs a heavy-duty application of common sense, powerful will and enlightened "generalship." However, this comfort with high risk and volatility may result in Eight setting a pace and a strategy that leave the rest of the organization breathless.
Nine: Mediator Motivated to create and maintain interpersonal harmony; incorporates others' agendas and opinions into decision-making process; seeks a comfortable living and working environment; steady, adaptable and easy-going; understands all points of view in a conflict, but may find it difficult to set personal priorities; may become stubborn and immovable once a decision is reached.	Promotes acceptance of differences and mutual positive regard. Emphasizes teamwork, cooperation and collaboration as a way to reduce conflict and maintain good will. Believes in hearing all sides of a dispute before making a decision. Prizes consistency.	Vision tends to be global and big-picture rather than specific, and incorporates Nine's intuitive understanding of the organization as a system where the team is more powerful than the individual. Direction is set and maintained by consensus.	Creates an easy, comfortable, low-conflict, orderly, team-oriented culture where employees are given a clear understanding of their importance in the larger picture, and where all differing opinions are worthy of consideration and respect.	Unpredictable, volatile environments that demand rapid-fire, on-the-spot decisions are challenging places for Nine, who prefers to create a plan in advance and then put energy into working the plan efficiently. However, Nine excels at hearing and communicating what all stakeholders need to be made whole.

Chapter 3

The Purposeful Leader

This chapter introduces the role of men and women as *purposeful leaders*, the first of the seven faces of leadership. In this capacity, they help an organization to reflect upon and to understand the purpose of its work and the values that underlie how it conducts its work. How we *think* about what we do, after all, has a major effect on both *what* we do and *how* we do it. We'll also discuss the crucial role that the leader must play in clarifying the meaning of the work that each member of the organization performs.

A leader must undertake to help the organization and its members develop a clear sense of values, purpose, and meaning. In the absence of this clarity, the organization becomes de-energized and conflicted. My experience leads me to conclude that strong beliefs about values and purpose are keys to future success of any organization.

Values

The values of an organization describe its beliefs and attitudes, its guiding principles and philosophy. They identify what is important and serve as guidelines for behavior. Good value statements do not simply describe how an organization behaves—they are also normative, defining how an organization ought to behave.

Most corporate value statements are flawed, for they consist of platitudes that a committee generates in a one-day meeting, supposedly to reflect the preferences of the populace. Leaders fail to assign priorities to the list of virtues, and most lists contain apparent contradictions. Consider these antinomies, corporate values that seem to conflict:

> Revenue vs. Earnings
> Profitability vs. Social Responsibility
> Focus vs. Diversification
> Stability vs. Growth
> Individual Excellence vs. Teamwork
> Tradition vs. Innovation

Effective leaders confront these contradictions and synthesize them in a way that either removes the conflict or establishes the appropriate balance among different values. They adopt values that are internally consistent, rank them in order of importance, and get the organization to subscribe to them. Most importantly, leaders encourage the organization to translate values into behavior—for espoused values are not always reflected in actions.

Most organizations will share similar values, and indeed there may be some universal values. Anthropologists and philosophers have cited fairness, freedom, unity, tolerance, responsibility, respect for life, and love as examples of such universals.[1] Nevertheless, cultural norms and the needs of the times inevitably affect value priorities. The Puritans exalted thrift, while many aristocratic members of the European royalty during the 17th and 18th centuries favored profligacy. The French adopted *Liberté, Egalité, Fraternité* (liberty, equality, brotherhood) as watchwords prior to the French Revolution of 1789. After the fall of France in 1940, the Germans and the Vichy government substituted *Travail, Famille, Patrie* (work, family, country). The French restored the old motto when France was liberated in 1944.

---

1 See, for example, Albert A. Anderson, *Universal Justice*, Rodopi B.V. Amsterdam, 1997.

As another example, compare Thomas Jefferson's powerful value statement in the U.S. Declaration of Independence in 1776:

" . . . life, liberty, and the pursuit of happiness."

with these words from a similar document, the British North America Act of 1867, Canada's de facto Constitution for over 120 years:

" . . . peace, order, and good government."

These contrasting value statements illuminate the conservative (and perhaps more benevolent) orientation of many Canadians. In the U.S., by contrast, individual self-interest has catalyzed a remarkable entrepreneurial spirit.[2]

In organizations, we do find differences in value emphasis. Many corporations favor strong central control, for example. But Johnson & Johnson, with its array of over 194 companies, and the Swiss electrical engineering and equipment leviathan of Asea Brown Boveri, Ltd. (ABB) with its 1300 separate companies, strongly favor decentralization. The investment banking community prizes toughness, while many social service organizations place a high premium on compassion. The U.S. Army enunciates candor, courage, competence, commitment, and integrity as its core values, as well as the implicit value in the "officers eat last" axiom. In some other contemporary organizations (like Enron), the guiding principle appears to be "executives eat first."

Every leader has the responsibility to make the particular value orientation of the organization clear to all the stakeholders. But leaders cannot abbreviate the process of

---

2 Yet as Alexis de Tocqueville pointed out in his mid-19th century classic, the American stress on individualism produces rancor and tension that can isolate us and undermine our freedom, devaluing our belief in the very ideal of community and society. See *Democracy in America*, New American Library, 1991.

developing values by adopting simplistic statements like the Golden Rule, which only measures the behavior of others in terms of our own needs. After all, what we would have others do unto us may merely reflect our egocentric view of the world.[3] A better model might specify that we avoid doing to others what we do not want them to do to us. Or still better, that we treat one another as ends, not as means.[4]

Some organizations pass out the equivalent of stone tablets on which they inscribe this year's Ten Commandments (ten being the practical limit of what any organization can manage). Or distribute bumper stickers that piously proclaim the value of the month.

The Ford Motor Company, as an example, trumpets "Quality is Job #1." Evoking quality in this way focuses attention on an important goal, but it is no substitute for a value statement that provides broad-gauged guidance for behavior and decision-making. And for Ford, the torrent of recalls and law suits against the company in the 2000-2001 period suggests a serious lack of commitment to the quality goal.

The credo of Tylenol producer Johnson & Johnson (J&J), developed originally in 1943 and modified over a period of several years by a process involving many employees, represents the classical example of a value statement (Exhibit 3-1) The credo asserts clearly the obligation of the firm to serve the needs of doctors, nurses, patients, mothers and fathers. According to James Burke, CEO at the time, the J&J credo allowed the firm to respond quickly and effectively to J&J's Tylenol crisis.[5]

---

3 Laurence Kohlberg's model for moral evolution should be required reading for the leader. See, for example, "Moral Stages and Moralization," in *Moral Development and Behavior*, Holt Rinehart and Winston.

4 Both of these axioms are variations of Immanuel Kant's categorical imperative.

5 When another incident of poisoning occurred in Westchester County, N.Y. in February 1986, management recalled all Tylenol capsule products and replaced them with Tylenol caplets, incurring in the process a $140 million write-off.

Our Credo

We believe our first responsibility is to the doctors, nurses and patients,
to mothers and fathers and all others who use our products and services.
In meeting their needs everything we do must be of high quality.
We must constantly strive to reduce our costs
in order to maintain reasonable prices.
Customers' orders must be serviced promptly and accurately.
Our suppliers and distributors must have an opportunity
to make a fair profit.

We are responsible to our employees,
the men and women who work with us throughout the world.
Everyone must be considered as an individual.
We must respect their dignity and recognize their merit.
They must have a sense of security in their jobs.
Compensation must be fair and adequate,
and working conditions clean, orderly and safe.
We must be mindful of ways to help our employees fulfill
their family responsibilities.
Employees must feel free to make suggestions and complaints.
There must be equal opportunity for employment, development
and advancement for those qualified.
We must provide competent management,
and their actions must be just and ethical.

We are responsible to the communities in which we live and work
and to the world community as well.
We must be good citizens — support good works and charities
and bear our fair share of taxes.
We must encourage civic improvements and better health and education.
We must maintain in good order
the property we are privileged to use,
protecting the environment and natural resources.

Our final responsibility is to our stockholders.
Business must make a sound profit.
We must experiment with new ideas.
Research must be carried on, innovative programs developed
and mistakes paid for.
New equipment must be purchased, new facilities provided
and new products launched.
Reserves must be created to provide for adverse times.
When we operate according to these principles,
the stockholders should realize a fair return.

Johnson & Johnson

In September 1982, seven people in the Chicago area died after ingesting Tylenol capsules from bottles that were tampered with in retail stores and poisoned with cyanide. J&J voluntarily recalled 22 million bottles of the product, and J&J's market share of analgesics dropped from 35 percent to 8 percent. But three months later, Tylenol was back on the shelves with a tamper-resistant package, and the company regained 80 percent of its lost sales.

Similar commitment to "patients first" as a guiding principle for 15 years has enabled Northwestern Memorial Hospital in Chicago to achieve a reputation as one of the country's best-managed healthcare institutions. Under the leadership of CEO Gary Mecklenburg and COO Kathleen Murray, the organization continues to excel in a challenging healthcare environment.

The performance of the V. Suárez Company, Puerto Rico's largest consumer products distribution firm, provides another positive example of the benefits of focus and commitment to explicit values. Founded in 1945 and then led for many years by Diego Suárez, the company is now headed by third-generation executive Diego Suárez, Jr. The foundation of the firm's rise to prominence has been customer service. In the words of the founder Don Suárez Alvarez, "*Nuestros clientes son la sangre que le da la vida a esta empresa.*" (Our customers are the lifeblood of the company.) By treating customers and suppliers with respect, the firm has achieved a leading position in most of its markets (including a remarkable 56% share of the beer-distribution segment).

When values fail

Most organizations publish statements that proudly decree allegiance to values like honesty, integrity, community, teamwork, customer satisfaction, and excellence. There appears to be, in other words, little difference from one organization to another in what management embraces as corporate values. Regrettably, however, some organizations act in ways that are not congruent with their alleged values. Their behavior seems more to be driven by values like winning, profit, and growth at any cost.

Consider the unfortunate management of the asbestos problem by Johns-Manville, a company that manufactured a wide range of insulation products. Although evidence of asbestos insulation toxicity was available as early as the 1940s, executives ignored the mounting data. The company performed little research and took few initiatives to educate the customer to the asbestos hazard. Class-action suits by workers with cancer eventually forced the firm to declare bankruptcy to control its liability.

Procter & Gamble's management disputed reports that women had begun to experience toxic effects from P&G's Rely tampons. P&G finally accepted the overwhelming evidence of product deficiency and withdrew its tampons from the market in 1980. The French bottled-water producer Perrier rejected culpability for benzene in its water in 1990. But when it admitted that filter failure in the manufacturing process had allowed benzene contamination, it reluctantly recalled 160 million bottles and never regained its market dominance. Douglas Ivester, CEO of Coca Cola, faced a similar challenge in 1999 when 39 children in Belgium complained of sickness they attributed to contaminated Cokes. He waited almost a week to address the complaints, and then suggested that children were faking stomach aches. Ivester later expressed contrition, but the gaffe contributed to his early departure as CEO and Coca Cola's substantial loss of goodwill in the European market.

Most recently, Enron, the large energy trading corporation, with revenues of over $100 billion and over 20,000 employees, and its auditor, the Arthur Andersen Company, one of the world largest accounting firms, conspired to falsify financial statements and destroy financial records. The result has been Enron's bankruptcy, the largest in U.S. history, and the value of the firm plummeted from $10 billion to virtually zero. All despite an Enron corporate values statement that exalts Respect, Integrity, Communications, and Excellence!

Why is the gap between espoused values and actual behavior so profound in some organizations? If integrity, for example, is a core value, how do we rationalize their failure to be honest with customers or with one another? The answer is that leaders have failed to create a culture in which behavior and values are consonant, so that when managers identify problems, they can count on support from the organization.

Culture (the combination of beliefs and behavior) is always a powerful driver of performance. IBM's shared values and performance standards in the 1960s and 1970s, particularly in the area of customer service, contributed significantly to the firm's leadership in computer hardware. As IBM's responsiveness to customers began to languish in the 1980s, however, it lost its dominant competitive position.

Strong values alone will not yield high performance. Nevertheless, history suggests that only value-driven or value-based organizations are capable of enduring beyond a decade or two—if their values and culture are congruent with customer needs, the competitive environment, and the regulatory climate.[6] The Catholic Church illustrates the stability of a value-based enterprise. Founded in the first century A.D., the Church has withstood years of turmoil and challenge, including hostile takeover threats during the Protestant Reformation by heretics such as Martin Luther and John Calvin. Regrettably, the values of the Church have periodically led to excesses such as the Spanish Inquisition and the persecution of various minorities, including the Huguenots and Waldensians. And the Church is only today admitting its failure to oppose the attempt by the Nazis to exterminate the Jews during World War II and to address disclosures of sexual abuse by its priests.

---

6 James Collins and Jerry Porras find that preservation of core values is one of the key reasons successful companies endure. See *Built to Last*, HarperBusiness, 1994.

If values and culture are not consistent with strategy, performance will suffer, and either strategy or culture must change. A leader can change the strategy of an organization with relative ease, assuming appropriate resources and competencies are available. Changing values and culture is a different matter, and it is often more practical to change the cast of players than to suffer three to five years of slow cultural evolution. [7] We'll address this challenge when we discuss the *adaptive leader* in Chapter 7.

Purpose

Values shape the purpose of an organization. The purpose of an organization describes why we are in business, our rationale for coming to work, our leitmotif, our dominant theme. Establishing purpose often will require hard work by the leader, for many organizations cannot even agree on the definition of the business. Is Budweiser in the beer business, the beverage business, or the consumer-products business? Is Amtrak in the business of railroads, transportation, or customer service? And defining the primary customer may be just as difficult. For an insurance company like MetLife in New York, is it the agent or the policyholder? For a prestigious teaching hospital like Massachusetts General in Boston, is it the patient or the doctor? For Harvard Business School, is it the student or the potential employer?

Leaders clarify these uncertainties and help the members of the community comprehend or define their mutual purpose and align themselves toward the realization of this purpose. Properly expressed, ideology—the combination of values and purpose—will answer questions like "What do we stand for?" and "What are we doing?" An ideology necessarily includes a set of clear and unambiguous values, like teamwork, honesty, and civility, that characterize how we conduct transactions

---

7 The Christian vision, as one example, took many years to displace the Greco-Roman vision in Western Europe.

(modal values), as well as a set of end-state goals, like justice and equity, toward which we strive. Many companies, sad to say, muddle along with little to guide them except a strong need for survival, and employees in such companies are often unmotivated and unproductive.

Enlightened leaders help their organizations arrive at an empowering expression of purpose. As one good example, the global pharmaceutical firm Merck expresses purpose as "Preserving and improving human life . . ." The Girl Scouts of the U.S.A. claims as its purpose, "inspiring girls with the highest ideals of character, conduct, patriotism, and service that they may become happy and resourceful citizens." Other examples of core purpose include Fannie Mae's "The American Dream," Walt Disney's "To make people happy," Mary Kay's "To give unlimited opportunity to women," and Avon's "The Company for Women."

While lacking a formal corporate credo, Aaron Feuerstein, CEO of Malden Mills, a manufacturer of the insulating polyesters Polartec® and Polarfleece® in Lawrence, Massachusetts, illustrates core purpose by his behavior (always the best test).[8] After a fire nearly destroyed the manufacturing plant on December 12, 1995, Feuerstein decided to utilize the insurance proceeds to rebuild the plant in the same location and rehire most of the 3000 workers. Almost 85 percent of the workers were back on the job by September 1996, and the company retrained the others. In support of his philosophy, Feuerstein observed that production in the plant rose from 120,000 to over 200,000 yards per week after the plant was rebuilt.[9]

---

8 Polarfleece® is a successful innovation in an industry noted for its modest commitments to new product development. Goretex®, produced by W.L.Gore & Associates; Thinsulate®, produced by 3M; and Nylon, produced by DuPont, were similar innovations.

9 Malden Mills is in crisis again, however. A weak economy and severe competition forced Feuerstein to file for Chapter 11 bankruptcy protection in November 2001.

The conventional attitude, advocated by University of Chicago economist Milton Friedman and others, is that the business of business is business—and increasing shareholder value is the primary obligation of the enterprise. But this parochial short-term economic perspective, which exalts net present value, internal rate of return, discounted cash flow, or shareholder value as primary measures of performance has led many firms to the brink of immorality.

In a memorable article, Supreme Court Justice Louis D. Brandeis reminds us of the purpose of a profession.[10]

- It is an occupation which is pursued largely for others and not merely for one's self
- It is an occupation in which the amount of financial return is not the accepted measure of success

Brandeis illustrated the importance of performing for others rather than for ourselves with his case history on Filene's of Boston, a retailer that grew successfully for many years. The cornerstone of its growth was management's belief that retail distribution was a social service ("equal in dignity and responsibility to the function of production.") This concept has origins deep in Western philosophy, as witness Socrates' observation many years ago that "a true professional, in giving orders to others, works not for self-interest but always for the benefit of others."[11]

Recent deviants from these principles include Archer-Daniels-Midland (price fixing), NBC TV (falsification of videotapes of automobile safety), and Prudential Insurance (fraudulent consumer-sales practices). GE continues to deny culpability for the pollution of the upper Hudson River in

10 Louis D. Brandeis, "Business—A Profession," *System*, October 1912.
11 Plato, *The Republic*, 347.
12 In December 2001, the Environmental Protection Agency ordered GE to begin cleanup operations.

New York by PCBs discharged from one of its processing plants.[12] And Sony hired public relations agents in 2001 to fabricate favorable reviews of Sony's recent film releases. Even Johnson & Johnson, which established itself as a paragon of ethical behavior in its 1982 and 1986 responses to Tylenol incidents, fell from grace in 1995. One of its divisions shredded documents that the Justice Department sought to support an investigation of J&J's Retin, a high-potency skin-care product; the corporation agreed to pay fines of $7.5 million to settle the case.

All of this behavior, I submit, is the inevitable consequence of the predatory global capitalism of our times, in which growth and profit are the primary driving forces.[13] This new ethos has substantially displaced both the Christian mythology of the West and the Confucian mythology of the East (duty to family and community). A more enlightened model for the corporation holds it responsible for a broad group of stakeholders: shareholders, employees, suppliers, customers, and the community.

In this model, the mandate for the leader is to balance the competing needs of the various stakeholders. David Packard, co-founder of the computer equipment giant Hewlett-Packard, asserts, "H-P does not exist to make a profit; it exists to make a contribution."[14] The Herman Miller Company, the $2 billion global provider of office furniture, founded in 1923, expresses a similar broad purpose: "Mere exchange of goods and services for money is not enough for us. We have a higher aim—to make a meaningful contribution to the people we serve."

The emergence over the past ten years of mutual funds that espouse broad social objectives reflects a similar de-emphasis of profitability as the sole purpose of an enterprise. Socially conscious investing began in earnest as a protest against apartheid in South Africa. Today, the Morningstar

13 A recent apostle of this creed is Gordon Gekko, who proclaims in the 1992 film *Wall Street* that "Greed is good."
14 *The New York Times*, November 18, 2001.

investment service tracks 64 socially responsible funds. These funds combine traditional financial analysis with a scrutiny of a firm's social and environmental policies. The Calvert Group's periodic social audit of 1000 firms considers environmental policy, workplace issues, product safety, community relations, military weapons contracting, international operations and human rights, and respect for the rights of indigenous peoples. Companies engaged in weapons production, asbestos manufacture, or tobacco distribution usually fail the investment criteria.

Companies that meet environmental regulations or six-sigma standards for quality, for example, can gain long-term competitive advantage. But virtue may have a short-term economic cost. SocialFunds.com lists 27 equity funds; only 11 of the group have beaten or tied the performance of the S&P 500.[15] Nevertheless, wise leaders understand that the mere attainment of short term economic goals is not enough –an organization needs a deeper *raison d'être*, a redemptive purpose for its existence. Regardless of what it makes or the service it provides, it must meet the test of utility (promoting the greatest good, measured in wealth, harmony, excellence or happiness), or virtue (promoting fairness and justice, carrying out the obligation to do the right thing). Great leaders infuse their organizations with ethical and moral dimensions that complement simple economic identity.

Recent examples of business organizations whose missions transcend pure economics include The Timberland Company, a leading manufacturer of footwear in Strathan, New Hampshire. Timberland supports an active program of community service because, according to company management, "We cannot measure how well we're doing without measuring how well the world is doing." And Robert W. Fiondella, Chairman of The Phoenix Cos., the financial

---

15 Roger Lowenstein, "Unconventional Wisdom," *Smart Money*, May 2001.

services firm located in Hartford, Connecticut, is explicit about the importance of community development:

"I try and bring some good things to Hartford that I thought would stimulate activity in the city, nurture a more optimistic vision and perception, and put our company in closer touch with the community in which we work."[16]

His local initiatives include waterfront reclamation and the sponsorship of the Special Olympics World Summer Games.

A number of organizations avoid completely the emphasis on profit by focusing explicitly on social purpose. Notable in this category is the Salvation Army, with a ministry concerned with "soup, soap, and salvation." Its work force of two million serves 30 million people each year, and raises over $2 billion annually in contributions.[17]

The meaning of work

Many organizations are intellectually and emotionally impoverished because their members cannot find meaning in their day-to-day activities. Often their mutual disdain for what they do is all that unites them. The effective leader understands this risk and takes steps to insure that the values and purpose of the organization are consonant with what its members deem to be important.

All men and women need to find meaning and purpose. Otherwise they condemn themselves to a schizophrenic separation between their personal and professional lives.

One need only look at Studs Terkel's extraordinary anthology of interviews with working men and women to understand the deep malaise that many experience.[18] Terkel writes:

16 John Steinbreder, "Hartford Rising," *Sky*, September 1998.
17 Robert A. Watson, *The Most Effective Organization in the U.S.*, Crown Business, 2001.
18 Studs Terkel, *Working*, The New Press, 1974.

The blue-collar blues is no more bitterly sung than the white collar moan. "I'm a machine," says the spot welder. "I'm caged," says the bank teller and echoes the hotel clerk. "I'm a mule," says the steel worker. "A monkey can do what I do," says the receptionist. "I'm less than a farm implement," says the migrant worker. "I'm an object," says the high-fashion model. Blue collar, and white, call upon the identical phrase: "I'm a robot."

Brazilian Sebastião Salgado trained originally as a development economist, has made an important contribution to the understanding of the importance of meaningful work through the medium of photography. His 1993 opus, *Workers*, comprises 250 images of men and women doing their work in a variety of dehumanizing circumstances, such as deep pit gold mines in Brazil, oil wells in Kuwait, and sugar cane fields in Cuba.[19]

Salgado's images are remarkable in two senses. First of all, they reveal the grim contrast between the working conditions that professional men and women experience in developed countries, and the working conditions of most people in the Third World. Yet despite degrading and dehumanizing conditions, some workers in Salgado's photographs express deep pride and dignity. (see Exhibit 3-2) Salgado describes the attitude of the fisherwomen of Vigo in Galicia:

They are strong and handsome, even sensual, these peasant women of the sea who hoe the land at low tide. They are peasants because fishing for almejas, which are like clams, is not fishing but harvesting. The almeja is cultivated, left to grow on the bottom of the sea near the coast. Then, with October and the largest tides of the year, the water recedes one or two miles from the shoreline, and women come to pick their crops every day for two to three months.

The women do not belong to this world. Their feet stand on the muddy flats of the ria, the wind blows in their face. What can they remember, these peasant women of the waters, as they pull the fruit of the sea at low tide? Why do they smile?

---

19 Salgado's recent series of photographs depicts the plight of the homeless in Brazil.

They smile, we infer, because they have pride in their work—they have found meaning and significance in what they do. Psychoanalyst Viktor Frankl, a survivor of the German

Exhibit 3.2 Coal Workers in Dhanbad, India

concentration camps in World War II, makes clear the overarching importance of this motivation:

To live is to suffer; to survive is to find meaning in the suffering. No man can tell another what his purpose is. Each must find out for himself and accept the responsibility that his answer prescribes.[20]

The leader who endeavors to raise the morale and energy level of the organization must understand that lack of meaning in the work that people do will corrode the fabric of the community. One source of meaning can be the purpose of the organization (achieving world peace, say). A noble purpose can inspire men and women, reassure them that they are adding value. But not all organizations have noble purpose in this same sense.

---

20 Viktor E. Frankl, *Man's Search for Meaning*, Washington Square Press, 1963. Frankl goes on to assert that man must maintain a "tragic optimism."

Consider the plight of Sisyphus, described in the classic Greek myth. The Gods have condemned Sisyphus, King of Corinth, to the underworld for various transgressions. His specific punishment is to spend his days rolling a large rock up a hill. When he gets it to the top, the rock rolls back down to the bottom. He repeats his act of physical heroism again and again. French novelist Albert Camus asserts that Sisyphus is happy.[21] How can we understand this conclusion? Does Sisyphus' project have meaning because it does not end? In his perseverance does Sisyphus obtain a curious revenge upon the Gods? As a metaphor for life, Sisyphus' story suggests that we can derive meaning from any task—even rolling stones. Repetitive work can create a ritual that gives great satisfaction, as do most rituals. The prerequisite is that we invest ourselves fully in the experience.

We can go back several thousand years and find the same theme. In the *Bhagavad Gita*, the famous scripture imbedded in the Hindu epic, the *Mahabharata*, the Divine Lord Krishna addresses the saintly warrior Arjuna, caught in a vortex of self-doubt, confusion, and despair as he prepares for battle against his kin:[22]

You have the right to work, but for the work's sake alone. You have no rights to the fruits of work. Desire for the fruits of work must never be your motive in working. Work done with anxiety about results is far inferior to work done without such anxiety, in the calm of self-surrender. They who work selfishly for results are miserable.[23]

Miguel de Cervantes' 17th century saga of *Don Quixote* shows us how individuals can develop meaning. Alonso Quijana is a gaunt country gentleman who lives in the Spanish

---

21 Albert Camus, *The Myth of Sisyphus*, Penguin Books, 1975.
22 Swami Prabhavananda and Christopher Isherwood, trans., *The Song of God*, New American Library, 1944.
23 This is often a difficult perspective for disciples of the capitalist religion of the West to understand.

province of La Mancha. Believing that he has been called upon to redress the wrongs of the world, he changes his name and accepts a knighthood bestowed upon him by an innkeeper whose hostelry he mistakes for a castle. Choosing the simple peasant girl, Aldonza Lorenzo, for his lady love, he renames her Dulcinea and takes the peasant Sancho Panza as his squire. Setting off together they encounter giants (windmills), armies (flocks of sheep), and oppressed gentlemen (galley slaves). Ultimately disillusioned, Quixote returns to La Mancha.

How can we not admire the Don? Coming from a nameless village, he invents his life, invents names for the places he visits and the people he meets. He creates and enlivens his world, giving himself noble purpose. He tells his own story and infuses it with meaning. Leaders must urge the members of their own organizations to tell their own stories about what they do.

Purposeful leaders are sources of motivation and inspiration for members of their organizations in two ways.

- They make it clear that collectively the enterprise has significant purpose. *What* men and women do, in other words, is an important element in the development of meaning. (DuPont, for example, proclaims that they produce "better things for better living through chemistry.") Leaders make sense of what the organization is doing and convey that sense to the stakeholders.

- They stress that, as a member of the community, *how* an individual works is critical—for example, developing excellence in the techniques associated with his or her craft or profession, or collaborating creatively with others. This can then be another source of meaning for the individual.

The purposeful leader attends to values, purpose, and meaning. These are the foundations upon which a successful organization will base its daily activities and its long-term plan.

But it is not enough for an organization to be highly-principled, to have a strong value system and culture, and to have defined a compelling purpose. The effective leader helps the organization develop a vision for the future and a clear set of strategies for realizing this vision. In the next chapter we turn to this challenge as we explore the role of the *visionary leader*.

Chapter 4

The Visionary Leader

Hold fast to dreams
For if dreams die
Life is a broken-winged bird
That cannot fly.
—Langston Hughes

Men and women as purposeful leaders have satisfied the first part of the leadership challenge. Their next challenge is to function as *visionary leaders*, as they help the organization develop a clear picture of the future and how it expects to position itself in that future. Visionary leaders identify a customer need to be met, a technology that must be developed, an injustice to be redressed, a change that is about to alter our world, or an opportunity waiting to be seized.

A vision represents an ideal end state; it describes where we want to go as an organization, and it implies a set of principles that will govern how we'll get there. Louis Gerstner, IBM's CEO, achieved wide notoriety in July 1993 at the outset of his turnaround initiative for the assertion that "the last thing IBM needs right now is a vision,"[1] and Gerstner later noted, "we needed to save the company economically." But in the Spring of 1996, having completed his program of damage control, his position altered: "What IBM needs most right now is a vision." And the vision that ensued repositioned

---

1 IBM Annual Report, 1996.

IBM as an integrated computer services company using an open systems strategy and a networked model of computing.

Like a value statement, any vision statement must be simple, clear, and easy to understand. It should be action-oriented and act as a plumb line against which decisions and resource allocations can be assessed. Consider Eastman Kodak's vision "to be the world leader in imaging." Or financial service company First Data's vision "Every client recommends First Data." Or Baxter International's "Become the global leader in providing critical therapies for individuals with life-threatening conditions."

The time horizon for a vision may be five years, ten years, or longer. Konosuke Matsushita, founder of the Japanese-based global electronics firm that bears his name, is noted for his farsightedness. In May 1932 he shared with his 162 employees the long-term vision embedded in his 250-year business plan. Broken into 25-year segments, the plan committed to "foster progress, promote the welfare of society, and further world development." But no visions are immutable; they evolve and change shape as we begin to realize them.[2]

Leaders rarely select a particular vision as the result of detailed calculations or the application of a particular mathematical algorithm. The leader more often must call upon creativity and intuition to reveal the possibility of a particular desirable future, a better world. And there may be many attractive end states for any organization. Thus, success can be the result of adhering to a single product business model (Boeing's commitment since 1916 to commercial aircraft manufacture[3]), multiproduct diversity (3M's dedication since 1902 to its core technologies in adhesives and abrasives) or

---

2 Like a sloop sailing into the wind, frequent tacks (changes in strategy) will be needed to reach the mark. Similarly, in the future of any organization, there are marks beyond marks, visions beyond visions, and the leader must often change course to reach the destination.

3 Boeing has maintained corporate offices in Seattle, Washington, since its founding as a builder of wooden seaplanes. But it has now renewed its emphasis on

business diversity (GE's continuing adaptation since its founding in 1892 as a manufacturer of electrical equipment[4]).

Visions empower and energize. Consider the fable of *The Man Who Planted Trees*.[5] Laboring in solitude, Provençal farmer Elzéard Bouffier vows to plant 100 acorns a day in the desolate countryside. After three years, he has started 100,000 oak seedlings, shifting occasionally to beeches and birches. He works steadfastly at this endeavor throughout his lifetime—and he transforms the barren land into a verdant countryside of meadows and pastures. In this information age, creative leaders have a similar transformative capability.

We see similar vision in the work of Herbert Johnson, a horticulturalist who assumed responsibility in 1953 for transforming the Jamaica Bay Wildlife Refuge in New York City from a deteriorating airfield and city dump into a magnificent natural park. Johnson planted hundreds of trees and plants and created a natural home for migratory birds and waterfowl. The Refuge is now one of the most important wild life sanctuaries in the Northeast U.S., visited by more than 100,000 people annually.

Great visions appeal to both mind and heart, and the creative process of crafting a vision often draws upon the metarational or intuitive dimension. Jules Henri Poincaré, the famous French mathematician, almost invariably needed to precede his insights with a phase of conscious incubation. He observed that after having spent 15 days working unsuccessfully on a problem, "One evening, contrary to my custom, I drank black coffee and could not sleep. Ideas rose in crowds; I felt them collide until pairs interlocked, so to speak, making

---

diversification into finance and other unrelated businesses, and announced in early 2001 a decision to abandon Seattle as its corporate headquarters in favor of Chicago, Illinois.

4 Almost 50 percent of GE's income now comes from financial services!

5 Jean Giono, *The Man Who Planted Trees*, Chelsea Publishing Co., 1985.

stable combinations." By morning, Poincaré had the solution and quickly wrote it down.

The process of illumination can sometimes be observed consciously. Consider the 19th century German chemist Friedrich August Kekulé describing a dream in which he solves the configuration of the benzene molecule: "Again the atoms were gamboling before my eyes. This time the smaller groups kept modestly in the background. My mental eye, rendered more acute by repeated visions of this kind, could now distinguish larger structures, manifold combinations; long rows, sometimes more closely fitted together, all turning and twisting in snake-like motion. But look, what was that? One of the snakes had seized hold of its own tail and the form whirled mockingly before my eyes." Kekulé then says, "Let us learn to dream, gentlemen."

Note the paradox or contrast between the spontaneous, effortless, joyful illumination stage and the prior stages that require deep, demanding work, accompanied by emotional and psychic stress. For some, this stress may yield negative emotions that block creativity. Illumination demands serene attention; we must let go, observe, and even participate.

Industrial history abounds with anecdotes of the successful leader who defied the results of analysis. A creative intuitive leap provided the incentive for Robert Fulton's steamship, Orville and Wilbur Wright's airplane, Chester Carlson's Xerography, Edwin Land's Polaroid camera and film, and the Netscape's web browser developed by Marc Andreesen and James Clark. Conversely, we can point to Ford's introduction of the Edsel, RCA's ill-fated leap into the computer industry, and the disastrous U.S. campaign in Vietnam as evidence of the failure of rational analysis and documentation.[6]

Realistic visions, of course, do not spring from some mysterious inner fount, but depend on a deep understanding

6 World chess champion Gary Kasparov observes, "Chess is wider than just calculation. You have to use fantasy, intuition, and some kind of prediction." *Time*, November 6, 1989.

of context. As an example, leaders in today's financial services industry cannot be expected to make good judgments without considering recent trends: shifting demographics, new global markets and competitors, industry consolidation, product proliferation, changing distribution channels, increased state and federal regulation, and crises of confidence on the part of both customers and investors.

Ted Turner's creation of a 24-hour new network at CNN was not merely the result of a burst of inspiration. It resulted from the confluence of the deregulation of cable TV, the proliferation of independent TV stations, a decrease in the cost of video technology, and a customer appetite for television on demand. These trends, coupled with the lassitude of the networks, provided the opportunity that Turner and CNN were able to exploit.

How a leader thinks about the future has a profound effect on the dimensions of a vision. One of the key indicators is how he or she allocates resources in the face of uncertainty. Even if outcomes are certain, every leader's decision is biased, that is to say, non-rational. In fact, the "trash-can" model often applies to organizational decision-making: whoever shows up for a meeting contributes to the decision, using whatever data are currently available. When this happens, the outcome turns out to be "good enough," rather than optimal; the organization has satisficed (accepted a result that's good enough) rather than optimized the probable outcomes. Leaders need to make sure that they have access to all the relevant information that lurks in the corners of the organization.

The rationality of decisions is less transparent when outcomes are uncertain. Suppose, for example, that a leader faces four possible independent scenarios: N_1 (war), N_2 (peace), N_3 (inflation), and N_4 (technology breakthrough). For each of four different strategies S_{A-D} we can expect the monetary outcomes shown below.

Strategies	Possible Scenarios			
	N₁	**N₂**	**N₃**	**N₄**
A	$1 M	$1 M	$1 M	$1 M
B	$2	$2	$0	$1
C	$1	$3	$0	$0
D	$0	$4	$0	$0

Before continuing, make your own selection of strategy; then turn to the Appendix 4-A for the solutions.

In even the best of circumstances, leaders must work with imperfect information (perfect information has an infinite cost) and an incomplete data base. As a result, they must avoid the trap of demanding excessive analysis and recognize that all organizations tend to select data according to their preconceptions. They pay too much attention to recent data and not enough to averages or trends. And they follow the crowd in making decisions—it's easier, and it obviates the need for primary market or product research.

Leaders need also to be sensitive to their own risk profiles. Research in prospect theory, for example, suggests that we tend to avoid risk when faced with a positive outcome but seek risk when faced with the possibility of loss. For example, given the choice between an 80 percent chance of winning $4000 and a 20 percent chance of winning nothing, or a 100 percent chance of winning $3000, we strongly favor the second option. But given the alternatives of an 80 percent chance of losing $4000 and a 20 percent chance of winning nothing or a 100 percent chance of losing $3000, we strongly favor the first option! We weigh losses more heavily than gains, even when they are mathematically equivalent.

Other factors in making a decision, of course, include the current assets of the organization, the need for a win, and the consequences of losing (is the leader willing to bet the company on the expectation of an extraordinarily favorable outcome?)

Forecasting the future is a hallowed art, and confidence

in the ability to forecast no doubt predated formal planning. Astrology, for example, originated in Mesopotamia in approximately 3000 B.C. The Greeks often had recourse to the oracle at Delphi, where Apollo was believed to convey information (albeit ambiguously!) about the future through a resident priestess. The haruspices, monks in ancient Rome, relied upon the study of animal entrails to predict the future. Other diviners still use cards, stones, crystal balls, dice, shells, runes, tea leaves, dreams, and palms to foretell the future. Most contemporary leaders place little reliance on any of these techniques, but they can be seduced by the apparent reliability of computer models.

These new models and algorithms have enabled mathematicians to improve substantially the *precision* of their calculations. Unfortunately, the empirical evidence shows that their *accuracy* is no better. The famous study sponsored by the Club of Rome, using large-scale system dynamics, illustrates the limitations of computer models. The study predicted a world crisis by the year 2020 as a consequence of the depletion of natural resources and unconstrained population growth.[7] But these dire predictions have yet to materialize. We have discovered additional natural resources, population growth has slowed, and consumption has moderated. The model made the wrong initial assumptions and failed to allow for subsequent learning.

Regardless of his or her decision bias, every leader needs to face the prospect of an uncertain future characterized by inevitable change and unpredictability. Many have difficulty in accepting this premise, for some changes in the macro-environment, such as demographic trends, shifts in the global economy, and government policy modifications, often are geologically slow and therefore hard to discern. The slow pace of these changes encourages us to believe in stability.

---

7 Donella H. Meadows, Dennis L. Meadows, Jorgen Randers, and William W. Behrens III, *The Limits to Growth*, The New American Library, 1972.

But as we all know, rapid and unexpected changes punctuate our lives with alarming frequency.

Prophets have never successfully foretold the arrival of major environmental, social, political, and economic dislocations—and good leaders accord little credibility to contemporary seers. A mere ten years ago, only a prescient mystic would have confidently forecast the fall of the Berlin wall, the breakup of the USSR, the end of apartheid, the World Trade Center disaster, and assorted other inconceivable or unimaginable events. This is not to dispute that increases in personal income produce higher demand for consumer goods, that housing starts are a reliable leading indicator for lawnmower sales, or that an aging population increases the need for health care. These are situations, however, in which there is either a causal or statistical relationship involving relatively few variables.

All of our experience, then, tells us that

- The world is complex and chaotic
- Change is inevitable
- The future cannot be predicted [8]

We can find small, temporary, local regions of stability, but our system as a whole is unstable. Simple predictive models fail because they do not describe the behavior of systems that have many variables, such as the weather or the economy. And in these systems, the focus in recent years of chaos theory, minor changes in initial conditions conspire to produce astonishing changes in the end state.[9] Stephen

8 In 1931, Kurt Gödel, the Austrian-born American mathematician and logician demonstrated with his incompleteness theorem that uncertainty and undecidability are unavoidable. German physicist Werner Heisenberg established in 1927 the intrinsic uncertainty in our world with his principle of indeterminacy.

9 Edward Lorenz asks, "Does the flap of a butterfly's wings in Brazil set off a tornado in Texas?" Presentation at the American Association for the Advancement of Science, December 29, 1979.

Wolfram's recent studies of cellular automata, computer programs that dictate the appearance of cells in a grid, enrich this paradigm. Wolfram argues that simple rules embedded in these programs can produce complex phenomena.[10]

The paradox for leaders, then, is that while they cannot rely on prediction, they must nevertheless create a vision for the organization. The classic business planning logic (linear and deterministic) that most of us experienced in the early 1950s produced little but frustration. The massive tomes and their detailed analyses did little to prepare us for rapid discontinuous change, and failed to alleviate organizational stress. Leaders need to plan, however, in order to reduce anxiety about the future, to improve effectiveness or to increase efficiency—and to create the future of the organization! The visionary leader realizes that plans help give meaning to the organization; a reflective organization can gain greater awareness of its purpose through a planning process.

An early alternative to the bureaucracy of the planning process was the Delphi Technique, a collaborative process of technological forecasting developed in the 1950s. Few companies ever used the Delphi technique, but it was a direct precursor of the scenario, now considered to be a staple in the planning inventory of most organizations.[11]

A scenario describes how the world will unfold during a possible future. It is, then, nothing more than a story about the future, and managers have been telling stories about the future for many years. But until the application of the scenario process, heads of organizations adhered to the belief that a single story could describe the future—and that story represented a prediction or forecast. The application of statistical confidence levels added to the illusion of certitude.

---

10 Stephen Wolfram, *A New Kind of Science*, Wolfram Media, Inc., 2002.

11 The term was introduced by Herman Kahn at the Rand Corporation. See Herman Kahn and Anthony J. Wiener, *The Year 2000, A Framework for Speculation on the Next Thirty-Three Years*, The Macmillan Company, 1967.

The innovative feature of the scenario was the concept of multiplicity, the idea that many futures might unfold, depending upon the interaction of several variables, many of which are uncontrollable.

Royal Dutch Shell popularized the scenario technique in 1972 when analysts in their planning department alerted management to the possible consequences of an oil embargo, with supply control shifted to OPEC. The legitimacy of scenarios continued to increase, and most organizations now include scenarios in their inventory of tools. Working back from alternative futures, leaders can derive a set of strategies for achieving a particular end state or at least alert the organization to possible risks and contingencies.

The scenario has broad application in both the corporate and political arena. In 1991, for example, at a conference on the future of South Africa, a multidisciplinary team of 22 people created the Mont Fleur scenarios.[12] The four results included:

> The Ostrich Scenario. The ostrich depicts a government that does not want to face reality. An ostrich supposedly hides its head in the sand when danger appears. The ostrich does not want to see and cannot fly away, but has to lift its head in the end.

> The Lame Duck Scenario. The Lame Duck envisages a formal protracted transition lasting for most of the coming decade, like a bird with a broken wing that cannot get off the ground. And thus has an extremely uncertain future.

> The Icarus Scenario. The third scenario is one of macroeconomic populism—of a popularly elected government that tries to achieve too much, too quickly, like youthful Icarus flying too close to the

12 Rabbie E. Davis-Floyd, "Storying Corporate Futures," in *Corporate Futures*, The University of Chicago Press, 1998.

sun. It has noble origins and good intentions, but pays insufficient attention to economic forces.

> The Flight of the Flamingos. Flamingos characteristically take off slowly, fly high, and fly together. In this scenario, a decisive political settlement followed by good government creates conditions in which an initially slow but sustainable economic takeoff becomes possible. The key to the government's success is its ability to combine strategies that lead to significant improvements in social delivery with policies that create confidence in the economy.

The reality that unfolded in South Africa after 1991 conformed exactly to none of these scenarios. But the enunciation of alternative scenarios helped inform policy decisions by the country's leadership.

Executives who are distressed by the indeterminacy of the world will find comfort in the application of the scenario method, even though one scenario is no more or less probable than any other.[13] Scenarios are useful not because they help a leader predict, but because they highlight the unpredictable quality of the future. Ultimately they compel the organization to explore and articulate the forces that drive our markets, our industry, and our world. They encourage the leader to contemplate the implication of alternative futures and to consider contingencies—they provide the opportunity to respond to future events, even if these events are uncertain. Future uncertainty is consistent with our belief that we do have free will, that we can create a future and tell our own stories. In addition, the failure of prediction empowers us to act as if our own choices made an important difference.

How does the leader produce a series of scenarios that support the creation of a vision and plan for the future of the

---

13 A comprehensive overview of the scenario-planning process is presented by Liam Fahey and Robert M. Randall, *Learning from the Future*, Wiley, 1997.

organization? The process follows a simple logic that has three stages:

1) Identifying the driving forces

Driving forces are trends or conditions (social, political, economic, regulatory, and technological, for example) that will affect the firm, the industry, customers, and other stakeholders. For the U.S. nuclear power industry, the driving forces include rising energy demand, the economics of alternative energy sources, government regulation, and public attitudes toward the safety of nuclear power. For the automobile industry, the driving forces include fuel efficiency, auto safety, government regulation of pollution, and customer attitudes. For the healthcare industry, driving forces include demographics (aging of the population), reimbursement policies, and advances in diagnostic and treatment technologies.

Executives can often infer the effects of changes in demographics, such as ethnicity and age distribution, but understanding the effect of some other driving forces is much harder. The influence of technological advances is especially difficult to predict. New developments such as the knitting machine, the steam engine, the microprocessor, fiber optics, and the Internet have produced major economic discontinuities.[14].

---

14 Most technological change is both irresistible and irreversible. During the early 19th century, for example, English workers known as Luddites resorted to a campaign of breaking machinery, especially knitting machines, to protest against the unemployment in the textile industry caused by the industrial revolution. The Luddite movement began in the hosiery and lace industry around Nottingham in 1811 and spread to the wool and cotton mills of Yorkshire and Lancashire. The government hanged 14 of the Luddites in January 1813 in York, although sporadic violent outbreaks continued until 1816. But England's textile leaders, recognizing that change was inevitable, soon automated their mills, and both the cottage knitting industry and the Luddite movement died out.

The saga of Wells Fargo's legendary Pony Express offers us a poignant example of a discontinuity caused by technology—and an illustration of leadership failure to adapt. Established on April 3, 1860, as the Central Overland California and Pike's Peak Express Company, the Pony Express delivered mail over a 1966 mile route from St. Joseph, Missouri, to Sacramento, California. Operating in relays, riders were able to cover the distance in eight days (regular mail took up to three weeks) at a price of $1 (more than a day's wages) for letters weighing less than ½ ounce. But the Pony Express could not match the efficiency of the electric telegraph from New York to San Francisco, and the service expired on October 26, 1861—after a short and glorious life.

Driving forces are essential inputs to the plots that leaders develop in the second stage of the scenario process.

2) Imagining alternative futures.

Scenarios and descriptions of future end states require a logic, which derives from consideration of the driving forces, and a plot. To the degree that the stories represent the values and consciousness of the group, the story becomes the group's reality. And the group essentially recreates itself as it tells each story. Like any stories, scenarios may be perfunctory and drab. The challenge for the good leader is to make these stories inspiring and exciting.

As we have noted, forecasting future events in today's uncertain and complex world is a futile endeavor. But, as in physics, we can imagine them.[15] Scenario planning entails this very process of envisioning multiple alternative futures

---

15 The process of imagining unobservable realities is widely used in high-energy physics under the label of *gedankenexperimenten* (thought experiments). These were conceived because scientists could not observe directly the interaction of subatomic high-energy particles. Using this method, theorists in the 1930s predicted the existence of neutrinos. Frederick Reines finally detected the neutrino experimentally in 1956.

and conceiving other worlds. The curmudgeonly Scrooge might be our model—a man forced by Marley's ghost and others to imagine the dire consequences of continuing his current behavior.[16] Exhibit 4-1 presents some other examples of literary scenario creation.[17]

If the underlying scenario assumptions are too simplistic, even respected futurists can lose their perspective and wind up forecasting implausible scenarios—e.g., a unique 25-year long period of global prosperity.[18] Nor should leaders commit themselves to single future scenarios, because they are not realistic.[19] Leaders should always entertain multiple scenarios.

One scenario is usually evolutionary and free from surprise; it represents the continuation of the status quo. This is not necessarily the most probable story about the future— nor is it our intention to even discover the most probable scenario. In fact, scenarios encourage leaders to abandon the idea of finding a most likely future and substitute the idea of creating a best future. This demands a shift in mindset from reaction to proaction—the selection of specific strategies based on a consideration of what future would benefit us most, and what we can do to shape the world to our advantage. Scenarios are intended to raise consciousness and create

16 Charles Dickens, *A Christmas Carol*, 1843.
17 Authors Jules Verne, H.G. Wells, Robert Heinlein, Ursula LeGuin and others from the science-fiction genre base all of their stories on the creation of alternative futures.
18 Peter Schwarz and Peter Leyden, "The Long Boom," *Wired*, July 1997.
19 Dr. Pangloss, the incurable optimist of Voltaire's *Candide*, despite enduring many misfortunes, adopted a single scenario based on the assumption that the world was good and could only improve: "All is for the best in this best of all possible worlds." The target of Voltaire's satire was Gottfried Leibniz, the German philosopher and mathematician, who proposed the existence of a divine plan that was all for the best. Cassandra, daughter of Priam and Hecuba, saw only evil ahead, including the fall of the Trojan king.

LITERARY IMAGININGS
OF ALTERNATIVE WORLDS

4.1

Tlön, Uqbar, and Orbis Tertius

Jorge Luis Borges, the brilliant and ironic Argentine writer, describes the creation of an entire universe in this story. Searching for a particular quotation ("both mirrors and copulation are abominable; they multiply the numbers of men"), the author is referred by a colleague to an article on Uqbar in the *Anglo-American Cyclopedia*, but inspection of his own copy fails to reveal the relevant topic. When the colleague checks his copy (Volume 46 of the *Cyclopedia*), he verifies that it indeed it contains a four-page section on Uqbar. But other reference sources contain not a single mention of Uqbar, or the country of Tlön in which it is located.

By chance, some time later, the author discovers Volume XI of *A First Encyclopedia of Tlön*, and a friend suggests reconstructing all the missing volumes. Still another friend proposes a secret project to invent an entire planet containing both Tlön and Uqbar. By 1914 their collaboration has produced the last of the forty volumes of *A First Encyclopedia of Tlön*. Exposure to Tlön and the ways of Tlön, according to Borges, results in disintegration of our world. Tlön's language and history are eventually taught in all schools and universities, and ultimately our world becomes Tlön.

Einstein's Dream

Alan Lightman's wonderful novella, *Einstein's Dream*, illustrates the extraordinary results of altering only a single variable: time. The protagonist of the story dreams of a world in which time is an endlessly repeating circle, of a world in which time runs slower at a higher altitude. Or where time barely moves, or where people live forever, or where there is no future. In some of his other settings, effects precede causes, or people have no memories, or time moves more slowly for those in motion.

Flatland: A Romance of Many Dimensions

Another visionary is A. Square, depicted in this classic science fiction story. A. Square lives in a two-dimensional world. Imagining a three-dimensional world, he is proclaimed a lunatic by his fellow citizens and is interred for life. In *Flatterland*, *Flatland's* sequel, Ian Stewart reveals a more complex universe in which the idea of dimension itself is challenged. When A. Square's great-great-granddaughter Victoria Line enters the story, she finds "spaces with infinitely many dimensions, spaces with none, spaces with fractional dimensions, spaces with infinitely many points, curved spaces, spaces that get mixed up with time, and spaces that aren't there at all." Stewart shows how, starting with experience, we use analogy and abstraction to imagine new worlds.

awareness that the organization must prepare itself for a large number of possible alternatives.[20]

Even in the 16th century, Niccolò Machiavelli understood the importance of rehearsal, of thinking through alternatives:

If the enemy were on that hill and we found ourselves here with our army, which of us would have the advantage? How could we safely approach him maintaining our order? If we wished to retire, what ought we to do? If they retired, how should we follow them? And he put before them as they went along all the contingencies that might happen to any army, heard their opinion, gave his own, fortifying it by argument; so that thanks to these constant reflections there could never have happened any incident when actually leading his armies for which he was not prepared.[21]

3) Selecting a desirable end state (vision).

The third stage in the scenario process is the selection of a desirable end state—a condition that the organization will strive to achieve. The leader and his organization will select this end state, or vision for the enterprise, after considering the alternative futures that have been identified in stage two of the process. Working back from the future, the organization can then identify the present actions (the programs) necessary to achieve the vision.

Managers often misunderstand this process of developing a vision. The classic story describes the chief executive who arrives on Monday morning with a proclamation: "We will be the industry leader!" The accompanying goals are typically unrealistic (increase sales and earnings by 50 percent, for example). As a result, the disbelieving staff adopts a posture of malicious compliance, appearing to enact programs that

---

20 A truly prescient leader of the Pony Express might have envisioned scenarios that included the advent of not only telegraph service (dominated by Western Union for many years), but Western Union's successor, AT&T (telephone service), and even the introduction of wireless technology in the 1960s.

21 Niccolò Machiavelli, *The Art of War*, 1513.

fulfill the goals but in fact are irrelevant or futile. When the organization falls short of its targets, the players are punished and the process is discredited. But—if a significant number of key staff participate in a scenario process, a shared vision and common foundation for strategy selection can result.[22]

Scenarios force leaders to focus externally, on their industry, markets, customers, and competitors, as well as internally on programs, functions, and structure. They protect against dangerous simplifications, they respect the intrinsic complexity of our universe, and they clarify relationships, priorities, and opportunities. Properly used, the scenario process defers the selection of a best end state until the leader and his or her colleagues have explored the implications of other possible realities.

In the corporate world, regrettably, only a few leaders ever develop realistic visions—Henry Ford at Ford Motor, Edwin Land at Polaroid, and Bill Gates at Microsoft come to mind as exceptions. The rest are content with either slogans or simple statements of economic goals (more revenue or profit). As a result, leaders with vision can give any organization a significant competitive edge.

Leaders can apply the scenario process to any situation:

- *The Federal Reserve System* The Board of Governors explored the consequences of a potential change in political leadership and, at a more immediate level, the short—and long-term impacts of changes in federal funds rates and money supply on economic growth and inflation. The four scenarios identified were the following:

---

22 The surrealists use a shared process to produce what artist and writer André Breton entitled "The Exquisite Corpse." Groups of artists in this process collaborated sequentially to create either poems or works or art. Breton observes, "What exalted us in these productions was, indeed, the conviction that come what might, they bore the mark of something that could not be begotten by one mind alone, and that they were endowed in a much greater measure with the power of *drift*."

1) Up, up, and away (lower unemployment, growth at 5-6%, consumer debt at 15% of disposable income, increased spending on technology)
2) Stormy weather (economic clearing with occasional sun)
3) Beltway blues (stagnation produced by legislative gridlock)
4) Apocalypse (economic recession or depression)

- *The Government of Puerto Rico.* Executives examined the consequences of changes to the current Commonwealth status of the Island to either statehood or independence, as well as the effect of changes in the important Law 936 legislation, which granted significant tax benefits to U.S. corporations that established manufacturing facilities locally. They also examined the impact on the economy of four possible scenarios:
  1) Reduction in unemployment to eight percent
  2) Enhancement of domestic linkages (e.g., between the financial and manufacturing sectors)
  3) A quantum leap in tourism
  4) Accelerated development of agribusiness

The comparisons showed that improving internal coordination between different sectors of the economy (scenario 2) produced the greatest improvement in gross domestic product, while reducing unemployment gave the next best results. A sizable gain in tourism proved disappointing in terms of employment, production and income.

- *Life and health insurance.* Executives in one firm developed three themes for the evolution of the industry:

    1) The evolutionary scenario: continued industry consolidation, changing demographics, multiple distribution systems, increasing importance of information, introduction of national healthcare

    2) The restructuring scenario: redefinition of industry boundaries, including the advent of strong competition from banks, investment brokers, and other players in the financial services industry

    3) The globalization scenario: increasing presence in the U.S. of foreign suppliers, while U.S. firms accelerate their entry into foreign markets

It's easy to recognize that none of the scenarios in these three examples is mutually exclusive—but they all suggest realistic possibilities that leaders cannot ignore as they plan for the future.

One useful corollary to the scenario process is the analysis of vulnerability to unexpected events. This analysis identifies the probability of future events and their impact, be they positive or negative, on the enterprise. The outcome provides input to events or conditions that the leaders must galvanize their organizations to either exploit or take steps to avert.

Scenarios raise the possibility of multiple futures or end states. The leader and his or her organization will select one or more and—working back from the future—address the actions necessary to realize a particular end state. Although few leaders successfully utilize the scenario process to develop inspiring visions, they can use them to select strategy—the allocation of resources to particular activities. Visions, in other words, are merely fantasies (or hallucinations) unless an organization commits time, energy, and money to realize them. This takes us to the role of the *strategic leader*, which we will address in the next chapter.

Appendix 4A

Decision Theory Rationale

The best strategy depends on the leader's values, rather than the mathematics of the situation, that is, how he or she chooses to act in the face of uncertainty (which is, of course, the normal situation). Decision theory suggests a number of criteria:

> ➤ Act on the assumption that the worst will happen (the Wald maximin model)
> ➤ Act on the assumption that the best will happen (the Hurwicz maximax model)
> ➤ Act on the assumption that all outcomes are equally probable (the LaPlace principle of insufficient reason)
> ➤ Act to minimize the possible regret from the outcome (the Savage model)

Those who are cautious (postal workers) will apply the Wald criterion (Strategy A). Rationalists (most managers), applying the LaPlace criterion, will select Strategy B. Bad losers (Richard Nixon?) will favor the Savage Criterion (Strategy C). Adventurers or entrepreneurs are likely to invoke Strategy D.

We can quantify the departure from so-called rational decision-making, in which expected monetary value (EMV) is the criterion, by using the notion of utility or preference. Thus, an EMV of $1 may have utility greater or less than one, depending on the utility function of the individual or organization. Important components of utility include the discount factor for risk (how much risk will I take to realize a given payout?) and the discount factor for time (how long will I wait for the payout?). Most of us are risk averse, and we would rather receive payment today than tomorrow.

Chapter 5

The Strategic Leader

Our plans miscarry because they have no aim. When a man does not know what harbor he is making for, no wind is the right wind.

—Seneca the Younger

The creation of values and purpose provides the answer to "what's important?" The development of an inspiring vision answers the question, "where do we want to go?" But the *strategic leader* needs to link values and vision by defining "how we will get there." This is the domain of strategy. Leaders as strategists lay the foundation for future success while competing in today's markets. This chapter will offer the leader some guidelines for strategy development and some organizing principles that can be applied to thinking about strategy development. Although many of these guidelines are couched in business terminology, they can be applied with equal force to the strategic needs of other organizations.

Strategy determines the specific direction in which the organization will move—how the organization will allocate resources to attain its desired end state. It is the road map to be followed if the vision is to be realized, and it links value and purpose with vision. If the vision changes, as it often does, the strategy must also change. Indeed, strategy must necessarily respond to evolving customer needs and competitive initiatives even if the vision remains constant. In many cases, in fact, vision begins to emerge only after an organization has tested its strategy successfully in the marketplace.

Strategy describes what the organization *does*—not what the organization *says*. Thus, the best way to determine an organization's strategy is to observe how it spends its time, money, and energy. Strategy, in my view, is simply a pattern of resource allocation. Reading strategic plans often does no more than reveal managerial intention.

Many theorists find it helpful to distinguish between strategy for a corporation and strategy for its businesses. The corporate strategy domain includes decisions about what kind of businesses to enter or exit, whether to grow by diversifying (by acquisition?) or consolidating (by merger?), how to finance the corporation, and how to deal with the various stakeholders. The strategic leader will take an active role in these decisions. Business strategy addresses the question of how an enterprise can best serve its customers in the face of competition.

Before developing business strategy, managers often analyze their strengths and weaknesses. But the strategic leader looks first *outside* the business at the industry, the markets, and the competition. Business strengths and weaknesses are meaningful only in the context of what is happening in the environment, what the market seeks, and what the competitors are doing. The first step is to understand the industry.

Assessing the Industry

Several recent techniques for organizing information about an industry are helpful. The most useful are based on the concepts of industry structure and industry lifecycle.

Understanding industry structure

An industry is part of an input/output system, as illustrated in Exhibit 5-1.[1] The industry transforms or adds value to raw

---

1 Michael E. Porter has graced us with the most comprehensive analysis of

materials, parts, or components provided as input by suppliers. The products or services of the industry constitute the output to the market. If the industry as a whole is strong relative to suppliers or customers, i.e., it has bargaining power over them, it tends to be profitable. The relative performance of any single business is determined by how large an advantage it can establish relative to competitors, and how much bargaining power it can establish with customers or suppliers.

| 5.1 | ORGANIZING PRINCIPLES FOR INDUSTRY STRUCTURE |

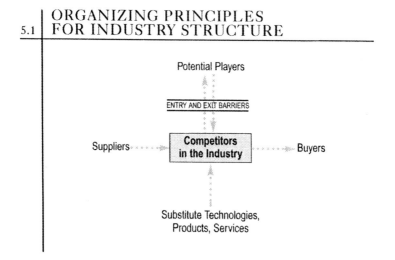

Corporations having excess resources often consider exiting into a more profitable industry. For many corporations already doing business in an industry, however, such a strategy is an academic issue if exit barriers prohibit them from shifting assets. Escaping from the industry may not be possible without paying a heavy price. Corporations also find that significant barriers inhibit their entry to other, more attractive industries. As a result, most leaders of organizations are destined to play out the hands they were dealt (or change jobs!)

For these leaders, a careful study of industry structure can provide vivid insights into how to manage more

industry structure and its implications in his *Competitive Advantage*, The Free Press, 1985.

effectively. Even in an industry exhibiting poor average profitability, an individual business can excel if it achieves or maintains competitive advantage. Let's consider the variables that determine industry structure:

> *Supplier Behavior.* The performance of competitors in any industry remains depressed if they lack control over raw material cost or supply.

> *Customer Behavior.* Buyers or customers tend to be strong relative to their suppliers under certain circumstances. Markets characterized by few customers (the defense market, for example) are notoriously unattractive to prospective suppliers, especially if sales to individual customers are large relative to a supplier's sales volume; a fragmented market offers suppliers greater opportunity to establish an advantage.

Customers who could reasonably integrate backward inhibit the tendency of suppliers to raise prices. For tire manufacturers, for example, the threat of automobile firms' manufacturing their own tires constrains profitability. Above a given threshold of price, quality, or service, customers seek a substitute for the industry's product. Examples of substitutability include aluminum for steel, wine for beer, airplane travel for train travel, solar energy for fossil energy. The incentive to switch is often high price, but social values and norms are influential as well (as in the substitution of bottled water for tap water, organic produce for commercial fruits and vegetables, soft drinks for beer and wine).

> *Rivalry within the Industry.* Intense and sometimes bitter rivalry among competitors can be found in industries that exhibit these conditions:

  o Many Competitors. Competition is intense when the industry is fragmented, particularly if the industry is growing slowly (petrochemical and heavy manufacturing).

o Slow growth. When the market is mature, firms usually can only grow by stealing customers from competitors.

o High Fixed Costs. When fixed costs are high relative to variable costs, firms are under pressure to use more capacity, most often by attempting to gain share. This fosters price wars that benefit none of the competitors.

o Undifferentiated Products. For commodity products or services, price is typically the deciding purchase factor. Unless switching costs for the customer are high, margins decline for all competitors, and the industry becomes stalemated.

o High Stakes. If the financial or strategic rewards for winning are perceived to be large, competitors will be loath to depart the industry, especially if the exit barriers are high—even if they are losing money (airlines and computers).

➤ *Exit Barriers.* Not only is the immediate cost of abandoning fixed assets or inventory a barrier to exit, but the delayed cost of satisfying customer obligations is also an obstacle to withdrawal. An economic analysis must consider how to absorb corporate costs that are borne by potential discontinued operations. In a number of European countries, for example, withdrawal from an industry is costly because of the government requirement to provide continuing economic security for workers.

➤ *Entry Barriers.* Profitable businesses are often

shielded from new competition by high entry barriers to the industry. These usually take several forms:

o Capital Requirements. The need for large amounts of capital is obvious when major investments in plant or equipment are a prerequisite even to entering the fray. The cost deters small entrepreneurs from entry. And even major corporations are prone to underestimate the total entry fee, as exemplified by RCA and GE during their ill-fated foray into the computer industry in the 1960s.

o Economies of Scale. Although economies of scale are often assumed to apply to manufacturing, they can be found in any functional area or activity. Thus, in the brewing industry, scale economies in advertising give Anheuser-Busch a significant edge over small regional players; in the information-processing industry, Microsoft and IBM realize comparable economies in R&D.

o Brand reputation. The implication of entering an industry characterized by differentiated or branded products is that customers must be persuaded to switch to new products.

o Distribution Channels. Access to distribution channels represents a major obstacle to entry, particularly in mature industries. Beverage and tobacco, drugs, food products, and many other consumer goods industries exhibit these barriers.

o Government Policy. Awards of monopolistic licenses (as in the U.S communications industry), or for that matter the assumption of a monopolistic position by the government itself (as in Argentina recently)) inhibits new entrants. Subtler deterrence can come from government licensing standards and policies, exemplified by the seven-year period of testing required before the U.S. Food and Drug Administration (FDA) approves a new pharmaceutical in this country.

o   Expected Retaliation. A powerful psychological barrier to entry arises if existing firms are committed to holding their positions and have substantial resources with which to defend themselves against intruders. This situation occurs frequently in capital-intensive industries experiencing slow growth.

o   Other Cost Barriers. Existing competitors may have lower costs if they have easy access to cheap labor, capital (for example, a government subsidy or tax advantage), or raw material, including energy. Favorable locations (proximity to customers or suppliers) may also provide cost advantage to early entrants.

Analyzing the industry lifecycle

The *product* lifecycle is familiar to most managers. Products are introduced, they experience increased demand, and then fall into relative disuse or are phased out (Microsoft's Windows 95 and Gillette's line of razors, for example). Hula hoops, bamboo rakes, buggy whips, parachutes, church pews, and men's hats illustrate this phenomenon. The *industry* lifecycle is less well appreciated. The premise in this model is that entire industries, like products and markets, also evolve through a lifecycle (Exhibit 5-2). During this cycle, industry structure undergoes major transformation. The lifecycle can last for just a few months or extend for many years.

5.2 | THE INDUSTRY LIFECYLE

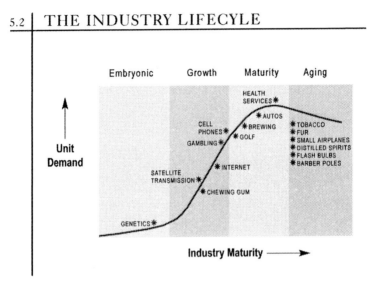

Although the number of stages is arbitrary, it is convenient to divide the lifecycle into four stages: embryonic, growth, mature, and aging. The duration of these individual stages typically depends on the industry.

Industries may abide in a particular stage for many years (holography has been embryonic since 1946, while textiles have been mature since the nineteenth century). Some industries or industry segments, on the other hand, like nuclear power, pass quickly through many stages.

When a product or service is introduced to a market and an industry begins to emerge, demand may grow rapidly. Total demand in this embryonic stage is small, however, and vacillates substantially. During the growth stage, overall product demand normally increases much faster than the gross national product. As the industry matures, growth slows to approximately that of the GNP. Most industries (and the U.S. economy as a whole) are mature. In the aging stage, demand grows more slowly than GNP and ultimately declines in real terms.

Specific segments within an industry, however, may have different positions on the lifecycle. Maturities in the sporting goods industry, for example, range across the spectrum. The market for baseball bats growing slowly, while the market for snow boards is burgeoning. The color-television industry is mature in the United States, growing in Europe, and embryonic in South America. Thus, although a business cannot escape its industry, it can improve position relative to the other competitors by focusing on high growth segments. Leaders can gain strategic advantage by understanding the characteristics of each of the lifecycle stages:

> *Embryonic Stage.* In the early stages of an industry, the relative growth rate is rapid and erratic, although unit sales may be quite small. Potential is hard to define accurately, because customer needs are only beginning to evolve. The number of competitors also is unpredictable, although the industry is easy to enter. Investment is low (many embryonic industries originate as cottage businesses), but variable costs are high.

> *Growth Stage.* Overall unit and dollar growth increases rapidly in the growth stage as new customers discover the product. Toward the end of this stage, however, the rate of growth declines and becomes more predictable. Attracted by market growth and visions of profit, competitors increase to a maximum number, although the increasing capital intensity of the industry eliminates some early entrants. Shakeout and consolidation characterize the late growth stages as competitive pressures increase (for example, because of price reductions based on economies of scale). Supply overtakes demand, prices drop, and weak competitors either fail or are acquired by larger companies.

As competitors accumulate market franchises and secure market share, new players find it harder to enter. The risk of entry diminishes, of course, if share can be gained without a direct attack on existing competitors, for example by finding customers with special needs. Although loyalty to suppliers increases in this stage, many customers will continue to seek alternatives. A few businesses may control a large fraction of industry sales, and market share begins to stabilize. The product line proliferates rapidly during the growth stage, and product technology continues to be a critical basis for competition in most industries.

➤ *Mature Stage.* At maturity, the industry grows at approximately the growth rate of the economy, although some competitors may grow by taking share from others. At least 75 percent of the assets of U.S. corporations are found in mature industries, including most primary materials sectors (metals, forest products, oil) and much secondary manufacturing. The potential for growth is well defined in this stage, and the industry behaves in a fairly predictable manner, although cyclicality often reflects imbalances of supply and demand.

Technology continues to be important. But since significant new product features are rarely demanded by the market, the technological focus shifts toward materials improvement and process efficiency. As a consequence, product proliferation usually stops in the late mature stage of the industry, as the recovery of product-development expenditures become more difficult.

➤ *Aging Stage.* Industries age when demand for products or services declines, often when the industry can no longer satisfy fully the changing needs of the market. Many competitors adopt rationalization strategies in this stage, withdrawing from unprofitable markets and eliminating marginal products.

As the number of competitors declines through withdrawal or consolidation, the market share held by remaining competitors increases. However, share distribution becomes more fragmented if competitors attempt to survive by securing a grip on a specific market or product niche.

Stable, long-term relationships between customers are an important basis for competition at this stage. Customers have little incentive to seek new sources of supply; their options become fewer in any case as the number of providers diminishes. But price sensitivity declines as the importance of product availability increases.

Aging industries fail to excite the interest of managers who have espoused growth as a primary virtue. Nevertheless, it is important to remember that numerous vintage businesses can be found in aging industries. Thus, even though profit margins for the industry overall are declining, the surviving businesses may be extremely profitable (the last icemen on the block). And indeed, many corporations celebrate their aging businesses as finally recouping investments made in earlier stages of industry maturity.

Forces within an industry rarely have an effect on industry maturity, with the exception of technological innovation. A classic example is the Japanese abacus industry, which in 1965 produced over 3 million units, the result of slow but steady growth since the device was introduced from China in the sixteenth century. Disaster appeared imminent, however when the cheap electronic hand calculator was introduced. World sales of pocket and desk calculators amounted to only 4,000 units in 1965, but by 1978 over 40 million units were being sold annually. Abacus output had dropped to two million units, although abacus manufacturers now forecast an annual growth rate of 3 percent. The slide-rule industry has not been so fortunate. Manufacturers like K&E and Pickett, who sold over 20,000 units per month in the late 1950s, have gone out of business, and slide rules are now considered to be collectibles.

The explosion of DVD sales in the home entertainment industry provides another example of the dramatic potential impact of technology. DVD players are rapidly eclipsing VCR recorders/players as the preferred consumer format. U.S. consumers bought 13 million units in 2001, a 49.5 percent increase over the previous year. Sales in 2002 are forecast to jump another 25 percent. The analog watch industry experienced similar transformation when new LED, LCD, and digital technologies were introduced.

Since maturation alters the characteristics of the industry in which businesses compete, we invariably observe a change in the way businesses compete with one another. In an embryonic industry, for example, price is almost never a basis for competition; customers typically buy on the basis of product features. In a mature industry, on the other hand, price is almost always a basis for competition. As a result, managers need to modify their strategy as their business moves from one stage to another.

Unlike managers, an industry may not mature inexorably with time. Some industries experience rejuvenation. The ski industry, as one example, was mature until the mid-1950s. Increases in leisure time and heightened interest in physical fitness, coupled with greater consumer affluence, conspired to increase demand. Market activity was fueled by technological developments in skis (wood, replaced by metal, replaced in turn by composite materials), bindings, and boots. Demand was sustained by snowmaking technology that extended the normal season by several months. The mature ski industry of the 1950s became a growth industry in the

1960s, 1970s, and the 1980s, but is now experiencing a decline as young people shift their allegiance to snowboarding. The bicycle industry of the 1970s enjoyed a comparable revitalization as a result of energy concerns, increased leisure time, and a sudden interest in health and physical fitness. Now, 30 years later, it too is mature.

From an economic point of view, no stage has greater value than any other. Businesses in the embryonic and growth stages represent the future of the corporation, but they demand high investment and often entail major risks. Well-managed mature and vintage businesses generate high profit and substantial cash. As a consequence, even though their own growth potential is limited, they can fund the expansion of businesses in earlier stages of maturity,

Defining market segments

What is the most appropriate way to segment the market? A number of possibilities present themselves, including

- Segment size and growth rate
- Geography
- Product type
- Distribution channel
- Customer type
- Customer need (application)

The most useful segmentation scheme recognizes key similarities in needs within groups of customers and key differences in needs between those groups. The differences between groups, moreover, should be profound enough to yield opportunities to differentiate products or services from competitors' products.

Defining segments based upon customer needs is a difficult process, particularly for consumer products where the basis of segmentation may include not only tangible attributes (specific features, function, or applications), but also customer demographics (age, sex, location), and psychographics (image, ego reinforcement). Industrial product manufacturers often have an easier task of segmenting based on needs, as customers frequently provide detailed or unique product specifications.

Managers should also be able to identify trends in the following:

- Distribution channels and patterns
- Price structure and movement
- Import and export levels
- Market cyclicality or seasonality
- Advertising and promotion practices

This information reveals to the leader how the market is evolving and provides guidance on strategy formulation.

A business can rarely serve all the markets that are theoretically available to it. To begin with, the needs of customers in different segments vary. As a result, serving every segment demands resources that exceed the capability of most organizations. Furthermore, a business normally achieves greater success by concentrating on segments in which it has advantages relative to the competition.

As a general rule, small, rapidly growing segments with few competitors are more attractive than large, stable segments already populated with tenacious competitors. In the beverage industry, for example, the high-growth segments such as bottled water can accommodate a host of competitors; large slow-growth segments such as coffee tend to be dominated by a few large players. Whenever possible, small firms need to seek attractive niches, that is, market segments that are defensible against rapacious intruders and cheaper to serve than other segments.

In most markets, customers place a high priority on value, that is, the product or service quality they perceive to get for a given price. The concept of quality is usually taken to include all product attributes (including service) other than price. But competitors may deliberately position their products to serve customers with different needs for product or service quality. They may provide equal value by selling a premium product at a high price (competitor C in the example of Exhibit 5-3) or an economy product at a low price (competitor A in the example). In the automobile industry, for example, General Motors positions its product line along the entire range of value, with Cadillac as the premium product, Chevrolet as the economy product, and Buick, Pontiac, and Oldsmobile (now extinct) in the middle range. Gillette sells both a low-priced Good News! razor and a high-priced Mach-3 razor. Discount merchandisers typically position themselves at the low end of the range (at or below point A in Exhibit 5-3) against department stores at the upper end of the range.

5.3 | THE PRICE-QUALITY RELATIONSHIP

The relationship between quality and price in a market is described by the fair value line; in markets served by unique or high-risk products (for example, jewelry or cardiovascular drugs), value is strongly dependent upon quality, whereas in markets served by commodity products, value depends strongly on price. The fair-value relationship often shifts to the right as customer expectations increase and competitors introduce new technology or reduce price to gain market share.

Competitors who position themselves below the fair value line are perceived by the customer as offering greater value (higher quality at an equivalent price or equivalent quality at lower price) and can expect to gain share. Conversely, the competitor who offers lower perceived value can expect to lose share. The strategic imperatives of low value relative to competitors are straightforward: either improve quality or cut price. Similarly, a competitor whose products are highly valued may increase price or simply allow market share to increase as customers switch to products having higher value to them.

Appraising the competition

Strategy is the art of deploying resources toward market opportunities in a way that distinguishes a business from its competitors. It follows that analyzing competitors is a crucial precursor to formulating good strategy. Nonetheless, such analysis is often implicit, incomplete, or lacking objectivity. Managers often assume that they know all about the competition and do not have to waste time on further analysis, that the information cannot be collected, or that competitors cannot be evaluated. Analyzing competitors is indeed time-consuming, and collecting information may be difficult, particularly if it is not available in the public domain.

Nevertheless, examination of competitors' current products, pricing, distribution, and marketing practices can reveal their strategies. Leaders can then develop responses to possible future competitor strategies.

Competitive position

Competitive position is a measure of the strength of a business within its industry. To determine the relative competitive position of a business, simply compare it with its peers using the key success factors for the industry, the qualities necessary to do well in the industry. The key success factors will vary by industry; some examples follow:

- Product features (personal computers, software)
- Product cost (beer, steel, paper)
- Product quality and performance (consumer electronics)
- Brand image (toothpaste, soft drinks, designer jeans)
- Customer service (home appliances, restaurants)
- On-time delivery (fashion merchandising, most consumer goods)

Empirical evidence has demonstrated that the factors that determine success or failure rarely exceed five; in some embryonic industries only one factor, technology, is important. Furthermore, the key success factors for an industry (the basis for competition) change as the environment in which the business operates changes. In the automobile industry, for example, quality and fuel economy are being displaced by design as a salient basis for competition (price continues to be important, of course).

Although they're not found in every industry, *leading* firms dominate their industry—they control the behavior of other competitors. IBM occupied this position in the personal-computer industry for many years. When IBM changed system architecture, software standards, or price, most competitors were forced to follow its lead. Dell is the new leader in the industry in 2001, with 24.5 percent of the U.S. market, and 13.1 percent of the world market; its direct sales model has allowed savings from lower PC-component prices to be passed along quickly to consumers. Anheuser-Busch has recently achieved leadership in the brewing industry, controlling almost 50 percent of the world market. As the low-cost producer, the firm controls price in the premium and super-premium segments of the beer market. DeBeers remains the leader in the diamond industry, with over 80 percent of the world's production. Microsoft and Intel continue to be leaders in their industries.

General Motors dominated the automobile industry for many years, until the corporation's insensitivity to consumer needs allowed German and Japanese competitors to erode its lead. A partial recovery of share in the early-1980s was again lost in the mid-1980s. Constant surveillance is the message. U.S. Steel, the dominant player in steel in the 1950s, committed resources to an old technology. Subsequent allocation of corporate resources to diversification amounted to a tacit withdrawal from the industry, allowing aggressive Japanese firms using new technology to take the lead. Montgomery Ward ceded leadership to Sears after World War II by virtue of its decision not to continue store expansion. And RCA's loss of leadership in color television to Japanese competitors is legendary.

By definition, an industry can have only one leader. And since leadership is hard to achieve and even harder to maintain, not every industry has a leader that can control the performance or behavior of other competitors and implement whatever strategy it chooses. More common is the leaderless industry made up of one or more strong competitors.

Strong competitors are those who have a wide choice of independent strategies that can be adopted without endangering their short-term position; they are relatively invulnerable to the actions of their competitors. In the computer industry, Compaq and Hewlett-Packard satisfy this specification. In the fast-food industry, Burger King is a strong competitor. Coca-Cola and PepsiCo represent the two strong competitors in the soft-drink industry, while GM, Ford, and Toyota are strong competitors in automobiles.

Favorable competitors are able to differentiate themselves, often in a product and market niche. Apple in the computer industry, Coors in the brewing industry, Seven-Up in soft drinks, and BMW in automobiles occupy favorable competitive positions. Firms in a favorable competitive position have a better-than-average opportunity to improve by selecting from several possible strategies. Their competitive mobility is limited, however, by the actions of firms in strong or leading positions.

Tenable competitors exhibit performance that may justify continuation of the business, particularly if there are significant exit barriers. However, the opportunities to enhance position are not obvious, and these firms consequently have a less-than-average opportunity to improve themselves. Nevertheless, if they are well capitalized, tenable competitors sometimes carry on business operations for many years

Weak competitors usually complete the lineup of players in an industry. The unsatisfactory market and financial performance of these businesses reflect significant competitive weakness—typically the result of high costs, low customer value, poor image, or inappropriate strategy. They must improve quickly if they are to survive, but in most cases poor management reduces the probability of a turnaround. As a result, they ultimately withdraw from the industry.

Portfolio analysis

Portfolio analysis was a popular tool in strategic planning for at least two decades. However, it has recently fallen into disrepute for being misleading or too simplistic; notions of core competence are currently held in higher favor. This is unfortunate because portfolio analysis, applied with discretion and sensitivity, can be a powerful weapon in the leader's strategic armory; it can be applied to both a portfolio of businesses (corporate strategy) and a portfolio of products and services (business strategy). The portfolio methods in common use include the growth/share matrix and the maturity/competitive position matrix.

Drawing upon the insights provided by the experience curve, the 2 x 2 matrix devised by the Boston Consulting Group (BCG) in the early 1960s was the progenitor of all subsequent portfolio analysis. The essential premise of this matrix (Exhibit 5-4) is that higher market share (greater experience) leads to lower cost. As a result, high-share businesses benefit from an intrinsic competitive advantage that can be utilized to reduce price, putting other high-cost competitors at a serious disadvantage. Alternatively, price can be maintained at the historic market level, producing higher profit and cash flow for the competitor with lowest costs.

5.4 | THE SHARE-GROWTH MATRIX

A corporation's most attractive businesses (the stars) are those with high market share in high-growth markets, where sales can be expanded without necessarily taking share from others. Stars exhibit strong and increasing profit and cash flow. Businesses with high market share in slow growth markets (the cash cows) also display good profit and cash flow, but their long-term growth potential is limited. Question mark or problem child businesses have small shares in growing markets—their futures are uncertain. Finally, businesses having small shares of slow-growth markets are uncharitably denoted as dogs.

The standard success sequence has stars ultimately evolving to cows, question marks successfully managed to become stars, and dogs being eliminated. The net cash outflow from stars and cows is reallocated to fuel the ascension of question marks to stronger positions in the portfolio. In the disaster sequence, stars degenerate to question marks and then to dogs, while cash cows mutate directly to dogs.

Managers often misapply or misunderstand the BCG matrix. For example, neither high market share nor rapid growth is a prerequisite to success. Some small share businesses are extremely successful (Steinway in pianos), while some large share businesses lose money (U.S. Steel in the 1960s).

If 2 x 2 is good, 4 x 5 must be better. In this portfolio model, developed at Arthur D. Little market share is replaced by competitive position, and market growth becomes industry lifecycle stage (Exhibit 5-5). Although competitive position cannot be computed precisely, it can be assessed with considerable confidence, as pointed out earlier. And although industry maturity is a complex concept, it too can be estimated with some precision.

Careful analysis of the situation is the leader's prelude to strategy formulation, for it is the externalities of industry, market, and competition that determine the strategy possibilities. The leader who launches a strategy based only on the strengths and weaknesses of his or her firm takes high risks. A business is strong or weak only relative to competitors.

The structure of most industries evolves dramatically over time. Thus, as a prelude to strategy formulation, leaders must develop not only a picture of the industry today but also a scenario for an appropriate future time horizon. The horizon

| 5.5 | THE MATURITY-
COMPETITIVE POSITION MATRIX |

Maturity Stage

	Embryonic	Growth	Maturity	Aging

Competitive Position

Leading

Strong

Favorable

Tenable

Weak

A
B
C
D

CIRCLE SIZE = COMPETITOR REVENUE

may be only a few years for volatile industries such as toys, software, or fashion but may need to be many years for forest products, electric utilities, or commercial aircraft, for example. Industries that are benignly competitive today may develop vicious rivalries as markets mature, new technology is introduced, or the basis of competition changes.

An understanding of industry structure yields insight into potential industry profitability. Understanding the maturity of the industry suggests likely future changes in structure and performance. Segmenting the market unveils opportunities to develop or enhance competitive advantage (implying in fact that the strategy of the business is preordained by the choice of market segments to be served). And understanding the behavior of competitors reveals their strategies, their commitment to the industry, and how they may react to alternative strategies, ultimately allowing the leader to establish a long-term scenario for a business's own success.

Formulating a strategy

Before leaders formulate strategy, they must select a team to participate in the process. Do not underestimate the importance of this, for *how* the strategy is developed may be more important than *what* the strategy is. The strategic leader always involves key managers in the formulation process, for it is they who will be responsible for implementing strategy. Without an investment in the process, they will rarely make much psychic investment in the implementation of the leader's strategic choices.

The first step for the leader and his or her team (and sometimes also the last step) is to hypothesize a strategy vector. Three possibilities are available:

- *Improve competitive position.* This is the vector of choice for most growth-oriented North American managers. It is also a natural choice for businesses in the early stages of an industry lifecycle. Later in the lifecycle, on the other hand, attempting to improve competitive position is likely to be unattractive (the cost will exceed the benefit) or impossible (stronger competitors may not allow it).

- *Maintain competitive position.* This vector is the natural choice for most businesses in mature industries. It by no means implies passivity; substantial investment and a long-term commitment may be required simply to defend a position against aggressive competitors. The average business runs hard just to stay in place, as witness the massive expenditures made by Ford (to keep up with GM and the Japanese)), Pepsi (to run with Coca-Cola), and Burger King (to maintain share versus McDonald's).

- *Withdraw or harvest.* Withdrawal from the market is the most sensible strategic choice if a business is weak relative to competitors and competes in an unattractive industry. When properly managed (assuming the decision is made consciously), this strategy, i.e., harvesting, may yield a very high return to the stockholders .

The strategy for a business in the first two cases entails these decisions: "Which market will my business serve?" and "How can I achieve advantage in this market?"

Almost every business will find that serving a particular segment or segments is more attractive than attempting to serve the entire market, unless overall market share is sought to achieve economies of scale. The attractive segment may or may not be one that is growing rapidly, but it must offer the business a potential competitive advantage. The most attractive market segment is not always the one that is exciting or glamorous; it is the one in which you have an opportunity to excel. It is the segment in which your firm's competitive strengths are greater than those of your competitors.

In the final analysis, competitive advantage can only be the result of low-cost leadership or differentiation from competition in a way that customers value. This differentiation may be achieved by offering unique features, functions or performance to customers, in other words by differentiating the product or the service. Those who are unable to differentiate in one of these ways are destined to compete at a disadvantage. If sustained over a long period of time, this disadvantage will lead to failure. As British naturalist Charles Darwin noted in *On the Origin of Species* (1859), each living thing finds and occupies through the development of unique capabilities, some distinct ecological niche. No two organisms can coexist if they make their living in the same way.

Low cost is critical in most industries, except in the early stages of their evolution (hand calculators, personal computers) or when image and reputation are important selling features (cosmetics, men's and women's fashions). But low-share competitors may not be able to achieve cost leadership no matter what they do, particularly if the industry offers the opportunity for significant economies of scale. In these situations, competitors must seek a competitive advantage through differentiation.

Differentiation on a non-cost basis entails finding a way to provide higher value to customers, such as product features, service, distribution, reliability, or image. This may allow higher prices and margins to be realized. If an improved product offering results in greater unit sales, costs may also decline, demonstrating that cost and non-cost strategies are often interdependent. Some firms (Caterpillar in materials handling, Philip Morris in cigarettes) have successfully invoked both strategies. Usually, however, firms cannot afford to do both.

Variance in industry performance can often be explained on the basis of industry structure and maturity. However profitable the industry as a whole, a more important question for most leaders is how to improve financial performance within their own segment of the industry – how to beat the averages. Profitability within industries varies considerably more than profitability between industries. That is, even in unattractive industries, certain businesses perform exceptionally well.

Why are some businesses more profitable than others? It is the combination of strategy and implementation relative to competitors that makes the difference. From a purely accounting point of view, this means having higher margins or better utilization of assets than competitors (turnover of plant and equipment, inventory, and receivables).

But from a strategic point of view, margins are higher than competitors' margins only if price is higher or cost is lower. These in turn depend on having better quality, higher market share, or greater productivity—all attributes that are driven by business strategy decisions.

Consider the performance of well-managed pharmaceutical

firms and well-managed retail druggists. They earn approximately equivalent returns on equity but use dramatically different strategies. Pharmaceutical manufacturers introduce unique, often patent-protected products that can be sold at high prices to a small segment of the market, realizing high margins as a result. Drugstores cannot, in general, employ such a strategy. Their services are hard to differentiate, for they merchandise the same products as other retail druggists, and their average margins are low. As a result, profitability depends on efficient asset management (high turnover) and cost control, rather than high prices.

The empirical data on industry profitability confirm the basic axioms of business strategy formulation. Leaders must seek to either find a market segment in which their product or service is highly differentiated (allowing higher price) or maximize asset turnover by marketing their product to as large a market as possible.

These strategic relationships are illustrated in Exhibit 5-6, an industry-performance map. A business can achieve high profitability (return on net assets) by differentiating itself from its competitors (point A), which usually entails serving a narrow market segment with a unique product. But equivalent performance can be achieved by a firm at point B which successfully serves a broad segment of the market with an undifferentiated product. Winners in commodity industries fall at the lower right, and specialists win by positioning themselves at the top left. Businesses in the middle region are uncommon, since they have succeeded in spite of their position as neither a specialist nor volume supplier.

Either strategy enhances performance. Thus, the business at point C can strive to differentiate by adding perceived value so that its products and services can be sold at higher prices (a marketing-oriented approach) or it can embark on becoming the low-cost leader through reducing cost across its value chain. Alternatively, it can increase revenue (better marketing) or reduce asset intensity.

5.6 | THE INDUSTRY PERFORMANCE MAP

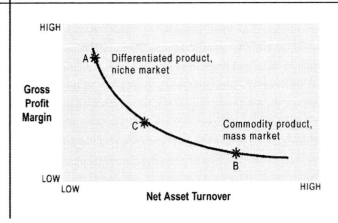

Every seasoned venture-capital investor and most division and corporate officers can relate stories of people who have come to them with ideas for products or services that are of higher quality, more efficient, or in other ways superior to anything on the market. Naturally, the budding entrepreneur also plans to offer this fantastic new item at a lower price than anyone else. Obviously, if a strategy could be employed to increase both product differentiation (unique features, for example) and process innovation (lower cost), business performance would be outstanding.

Occasionally a firm develops a "killer app"—a new product or service that establishes an entirely new category.[2] The electronic spreadsheet program VisiCalc, introduced in 1979, was a killer app, as was AT&T's "800" toll-free telephone call. The on-line auction site eBay may be another example. But conceiving the unique product or service that everyone wants is not easy.

Realistically, product differentiation typically increases both unit cost and fixed cost. Becoming the low-cost producer is often a long-term strategy that requires infusions of large

2 Larry Downes, Nicholas Negroponter, and Chunka Mui, *Unleashing the Killer App*, Harvard Business School Publishing, 1998.

amounts of up-front capital and a tolerance for reduced short-term profit. The Japanese, for example, are reputed to have lost money on motorcycles in Europe for five years after entering the motorcycle market there, but ultimately recouped their investment and came to dominate the market. Thus, leaders must select the more realistic choice for them, and follow one path or the other.

Many strategies are available, but only a few work, that is, achieve a rate of return substantially higher than the cost of capital. The others are prone to fail because they require excessive resources, invite competitive retaliation, or ignore the key success factors for the industry and market segment. This is not to say that risky strategy should always be eschewed. But remember that, even when successful in terms of sales or market share, the cost may exceed the benefit. Good judgment by leaders ultimately provides the balance between external constraints, the aspirations of the firm, and the risk tolerance of the managers.

Strategy selection is easy in embryonic industries (artificial intelligence, nanotechnology, genetic engineering, space travel), where no single competitor is likely to have a strong position. As the industry matures, however, the number of acceptable strategies diminishes, particularly if the firm's competitive position is weak. We refer to these as natural strategies—those that make sense and have a reasonable probability of succeeding. As an example, attempting to increase market share in a mature industry is usually unnatural—the reaction from stronger competitors whose share is threatened will destine it to failure. Even at the national and global level we can find natural strategies. Historian Paul Kennedy documents the inevitable attainment of an equilibrium global market share, based on a particular country's share of population and natural resources.[3]

Some leaders also make use of the concept of core

---

3 Paul Kennedy, *The Rise and Fall of Great Powers*, Random House, 1987.

competency, a set of core skills than can be combined to yield competitive advantage.[4] The classic illustration of this concept is Honda's extension of competency in engines to businesses in automobiles, motorcycles, outboard motors, snow blowers, snowmobiles, lawn mowers, and power tillers.

Let us assume that the leader has identified a set of attractive strategies. Which are the best? For the answer to this question, the leader must apply additional criteria. The strategies must be congruent with the organization's values and vision. Furthermore, they must evoke passion. The true leader finds the path that has a heart.[5] Strategies must not only look right analytically, they must resonate with the intuition of the leader and the management team.

Insightful leaders incorporate one other parameter as they evaluate possible strategies. A great strategy has one other subtle but crucial quality that resists quantification and rigorous definition. This quality is elegance. Elegant strategies are innovative, simple, clear, sustainable, and easy to implement. A prototype for elegance was King Gillette's introduction at the turn of the 19th century of a safety razor designed to accept only Gillette blades. He sold the razor at cost and made money on the blades. And we're all familiar with the more recent Japanese successes in consumer electronics, based first on shifting competition from service to reliability and then shifting it again to ultra-short product lifecycles. The Federal Express strategy offers another example of elegance.

In 1973, Federal Express adapted a hub-and-spoke delivery system that transformed the shipping industry. FedEx, whose revenues now exceed $20 billion, delivers over five million packages daily in 211 countries, using a fleet of over 40,000 vans and 500 planes. It commands almost 60

---

4 C.K. Prahalad, Liam Fahey, and Robert M. Randall, "A Strategy for Growth: the Role of Core Competencies in the Corporation, *The Portable MBA in Strategy*, Wiley, 1994.
5 "*Le coeur a ses raisons que la raison ne connâit point.*" (The heart has its reasons that reason knows nothing of.) Blaise Pascal, 1670.

percent of the overnight delivery market and just entered into a business alliance with the U.S. Postal Service. Why was FedEx able to overthrow the supremacy of United Parcel Service (UPS)? A strategic insight into the logistical benefits of a network (shorter and more efficient deliveries) enabled it to capitalize on man's inveterate tendency to procrastinate. (Arch-rival UPS, founded in 1907, still dominates the package delivery market on the ground. Using a fleet of over 80,000 cars, vans, and motorcycles, it now ships more than 13 million documents and packages daily.)

Stating the mission

The final and optional step in the strategy process is to articulate a mission. The mission is the sequel to the vision. Missions and visions are often confused. A vision describes what we want to become. A mission describes what we plan to do to realize the vision.[6] It summarizes the organization's strategy and goals, defines what it's going to do. As an example, John F. Kennedy mission statement in 1962:

> ➤ *. . . before this decade is out, landing a man on the moon . . .*

Or from the preamble to the Constitution of the United States, adopted in 1789:

> ➤ *. . . to form a more perfect Union, establish Justice, secure domestic Tranquility, provide for the common Defense, promote the general Welfare, and secure the blessings of Liberty to ourselves and our Posterity . . .*

Even the Starship Enterprise has a five-year mission:

---

6 Jesus Christ sent missionaries to convert the world only after he had enunciated his vision of eternal salvation.

> *To explore strange new worlds, to seek out new life and new civilizations, to boldly go where no one has gone before.*

Mission statements in the corporate world pervade most annual reports:

> *Raising the quality of health care in America (Aetna)*
> *To help individuals, groups, and businesses meet their financial goals by providing high quality insurance and financial services (Principal Financial Group)*
> *To create superior advertising (Leo Burnett Co., Inc.)*
> *To enable people and businesses throughout the world to realize their full potential (Microsoft)*

Many mission statements are either extremely abstract ("To increase shareholder value.") or confuse the difference between visions, missions, goals, objectives, values, and strategies. The leader must avoid these confusions so that all the stakeholders are clear about the intent of the enterprise.

To summarize

As we've already noted, the leader who dictates strategy, however elegant that strategy may be, runs a great risk of failing to secure commitment, or even worse, alienating the team, which will sabotage the desired outcome. As a consequence, the leader must give equal attention to the quality of the strategy and the process used to generate the strategy.

Most strategies evolve heuristically, that is, by trial and error. They begin to emerge with clarity only after the organization has explored a variety of options. But good leaders blend analysis and creative intuition to produce remarkable initial selections. Guidelines for the development of effective strategies are summarized in Exhibit 5-7.

Once leaders have gotten this far, they face the task of implementing strategy. At this point, the leader must energize the organization and secure commitment to the goals. This brings us to the next major leadership challenge—building a community and culture that will allow the enterprise to implement its strategy. This is the role of the *beneficent leader*.

5.7 | LEADER'S GUIDELINES FOR EFFECTIVE STRATEGY DEVELOPMENT

1. Planning process

Management commitment and participation are critical elements in strategic planning. Those who must implement a strategy must participate in its formulation. The organization will reject strategies, however brilliant, devised unilaterally by business heads or planners.

2. Plan for business units

Effective resource allocation requires that the products and services of the corporation be segmented into businesses. Strategies for these business units will then determine appropriate strategies for products, services, markets, and functions.

3. Data analysis

A lack of information rarely prevents a business from formulating strategy. The problem is more often an excess of information. Business managers require logic, analysis, and criteria to organize available data and facilitate the identification of clear strategic alternatives.

4. Differentiation

Many organizations attempt to apply similar strategies to each of their businesses. Different businesses, however, demand different strategies, which will produce different results and require different managerial systems.

5. Linkage

An insightful set of strategies for a business will not suffice to improve performance. Strategies must be linked to programs, schedules, and budgets. The responsibility of each function in the organization to support the strategies must be explicit.

6. Monitoring

Strategies soon lose their momentum unless implementation is monitored. The measurement and control system must close the loop between strategy and its implementation.

7. Management education

Internal communications will not be clear unless all managers adopt a common strategic language and set of concepts. The organization must make a major investment in education, for teaching managers how to think strategically is an organization's most effective management tool.

Chapter 6

The Beneficent Leader

No man is an island entire of itself; every man is a piece of the Continent, a part of the main.
—John Donne

The purposeful leader establishes values and clarifies the purpose of the organization. The visionary leader proposes an inspiring set of future goals. The strategic leader allocates resources to the appropriate strategies. The *beneficent leader* must implement these strategies, a task he or she can carry out only if the followers commit to the mission of the enterprise. The distinction between beneficence (doing good)) and benevolent (wanting good) is subtle but crucial.

This chapter summarizes the characteristics of a community, expands on the important role of leadership style in building a community, identifies some pitfalls for the leader, and presents some practical actions to be taken by those who want to build a strong community and culture.

Beneficent leaders are men and women who help the organization and its members achieve their collective needs and aspirations. Having values, purpose, vision, and direction is critical for any enterprise. But unless the enterprise *implements* its strategies, it will not progress beyond its current state—disillusionment will set in and performance will decline. Enthusiastic implementation can overcome the shortcomings of a deficient strategy. Ironically, in fact, the simple articulation of a strategy can energize a group.[1]

---

1 Karl Weick relates the story of a small Hungarian attachment on military ma-

The prerequisite to implementation is the collaboration of the individuals in the organization in concerted joint initiatives as a community. Beneficence, therefore, is more than altruism—it has a critical pragmatic function.

Creating a community

An important goal for any leader, therefore, is to move the enterprise beyond its mere legal identity as a corporation or a partnership. The ideal enterprise will behave not as a *company* but as a purposeful *community*.[2] What distinguishes a community from even a formal aggregation of individuals? A community is a group of people who choose to organize and be governed by a specific value system and set of principles. The statements of the U.S. *Declaration of Independence* illustrate this motivation:

> *When in the Course of Human Events, it becomes necessary for one People to dissolve the Political Bands which have connected them with another, and to assume among the Powers of the Earth, the separate and equal Station to which the Laws of Nature and of Nature's God entitle them, a decent Respect to the Opinions of Mankind requires that they should declare the causes which impel them to the separation.*

The essential challenge for all leaders, eloquently framed by Jean-Jacques Rousseau in the 18th century, is to "find a

neuvers in the Swiss Alps. A blizzard moves in, and the unit is apparently lost. But after three days, the unit successfully returns to camp. The commanding officer marvels at their feat. They explain: "We thought we were lost, and waited for the end. But one of us found a map in his pocket. So we pitched camp, waited out the storm, and used the map to find our bearings." The commander inspects the map and finds it to be not a map of the Alps, but of the Pyrenees. See *Sensemaking in Organizations*, Sage, 1995.

2 The Latin root of "company" is *com panis*, referring to the breaking of bread together.

form of association which will defend and protect with the whole common force the person and goods of each associate, and while each, while uniting himself with all, may still obey himself alone, and remain free as before." [3] In place of the individual personalities of all the members of the community (the state, the city, the corporation), Rousseau proposes a moral and collective body from which emerges unity, life, and will. By entering into this social contract, individuals lose their natural liberty and unlimited right to everything. But what they gain is civil and moral liberty and the proprietorship of all that they own. Rousseau's ideas strongly influenced Thomas Jefferson and the framers of the U.S. Constitution.

In order to achieve the kind of association proposed by Rousseau, leaders must create communities that meet these three criteria: strong boundaries; shared values, purpose, and identity; and trust and loyalty. [4]

- Strong boundaries

A community begins to form when a group of individuals establishes boundaries that separate it from its environment. Barriers to enter the community may include various credentials, characteristics, or values held by aspiring members. Barriers to exit from the community may include real or implied obligations on the part of the community's members to one another (for example, the U.S. Marine Corps: *A Marine for Life*).

Boundaries often exist as well between and within groups in the same organization, say between the marketing staff (who want to maximize sales), the manufacturing staff (who want to minimize cost), and the engineering staff (who want

3 Jean-Jacques Rousseau, *The Social Contract*, 1762.
4 J. Richard Hackman asserts that effective teams meet five conditions: they are real teams (not teams in name only), have compelling direction, have an enabling structure that facilitates team work, operate within a supportive organizational context, and have access to expert coaching. See *Leading Teams*, Harvard Business School Press, 2002.

to optimize performance). Individuals may also experience boundaries between their sense of self and their roles in the organization.[5]

The effectiveness of the organization will depend in large part on how the leader defines these boundaries. External boundaries created by prejudicial criteria, such as racism or some arbitrary definition of superiority, will limit the community's capacity for beneficial action. Internal boundaries, exploited by the leaders in a competitive or divide-and-conquer strategy, will disproportionately consume the community's time and energy.

- Shared values, purpose, and identity

A community offers its members meaning and higher purpose. Leaders create a climate of synergy and mutual support, reinforced by the sharing of information. Beneficent leaders strive to develop an overlapping consensus among members of the community, who ultimately need to agree about where to go and how to get there.[6]

Individuals in a community need to be heard—they must have *voice*. Moreover, if they wish to achieve alignment, individuals must experience one another with honesty and spontaneity. Dialog among the members of the community will eventually create a unique reality, a texture that binds individuals together. This is why effective leaders foster

5 Work at the Tavistock Institute in England in the 1950s, later expanded at the A.K. Rice Institute in the U.S., explored in depth the significance of boundaries, both visible and invisible. Tavistock theory also addressed the distinctions between formal authority, the authority sanctioned by subordinates, customers, and colleagues, and the power that the individual brings to the role.

6 Martin Luther King Jr. refers to this as a "symphony of brotherhood." Author Kurt Vonnegut differentiates in his novel *Cat's Cradle* between a karass, in which individuals have a strong connection with one another, and a granfalloon, a casual group.

communication and multilevel dialog and reward candor and constructive feedback.

- *Trust and loyalty*

Trust develops over time, and trust is the precursor to collaboration. The members of a true or fully-realized community will display a loyalty to one another that transcends self-interest, and they will assign equal importance to teamwork and individual excellence. The rapport and empathy in this environment will produce good for all. A recent example in 2001 was the offer by Southwest Airlines staff of cost-saving ideas for the struggling firm without regard to personal welfare, including taking on unpaid extra work and possible role elimination.

The interaction between leaders and followers

Effective leaders in a community maintain a symbiotic relationship with their followers. The leader's persona and actions encourage followers to behave in certain ways. Followers, in turn, reinforce or provoke certain behavior on the part of the leader.

Leaders may choose to view these relationships from several different perspectives.[7] The *structural perspective*—found most often in technologically intense organizations—emphasizes rationality, achievement of goals, and the efficiency of the organization. This is a restatement of Frederic Taylor's classic model of scientific management in which roles and organization structure are the critical leadership variables. The *human resource perspective* –often adopted in social service organizations—views the organization as a family; mutual support and empowerment characterize this perspective. In the *political perspective*—often

---

7 See L.G. Bolman and T.E. Deal, *Modern Approaches to Understanding and Managing Organizations*, Jossey-Bass, 1984.

emphasized in governmental and academic environments— leaders make decisions after negotiating with groups having different degrees of power. And in the *symbolic perspective*, leaders treat the organization as a stage on which each of us acts out a particular role; we seek meaning in myths, rituals, and symbols. Effective leaders typically adopt a blend of these perspectives.

Whatever the perspective, how the leader chooses to interact with followers—his or her style—is critical.[8] The choice depends on both the leader's self-image and the assumptions that he or she makes about the followers in the organization. We can identify three archetypes: the autocrat or tyrant, the reactive leader, and the participative leader.[9]

The autocrat or tyrant

The energy in this organizational archetype flows from the top of the organization downward, from the leader to the followers. But the man or woman who is a tyrant or a jail-keeper cannot lead effectively over the long term. Tyrants oppress. Jail-keepers coerce and control.

In *The Prince*, Niccolò Machiavelli advises his client, Cesare Borgia, to use power as a tool, asserting that the cultivation of fear is more important for leaders than the cultivation of love. Conquer by force, he tells him. Commit all your crimes against the people at the start of the regime. Be both a lion—strong and ruthless—and a fox—sly and duplicitous. The lion, Machiavelli points out, cannot defend himself against traps, and the fox cannot defend himself from wolves.

8 "It's not what I do, but the way I do it. It's not what I say, but the way I say it." Attributed to Mae West.

9 Plato, in his *Republic*, identifies five organizational types and their corresponding leaders: aristocracy, timocracy, oligarchy, democracy, and tyranny. Rule by an aristocracy of philosopher kings produces the best outcome, according to Plato.

10 Han Fook Kwang, Warren Fernandez, Sumiko Tan, *Lee Kuan Yew: The Man and His Ideas*, Singapore Press Holdings, 1997.

Good advice, perhaps, for those whose mandate is national (or corporate) security, but less compelling for those who aspire to leadership in contemporary society. Hyman Rickover, director of the U.S. Navy's program that built the Nautilus, the first nuclear-powered submarine, was noted for his frosty and autocratic management style. Other exemplars of this view are easy to find—for example Slobodan Milosevic, Yugoslavia's ex-president now on trial for genocide, and Lee Kuan Yew, the heavy-handed elder statesman who served as Prime Minister of Singapore from 1959 to 1990. Yew admits "Between being loved and feared, I have always believed Machiavelli was right. If nobody is afraid of me, I'm meaningless."[10]

In the corporate domain, Albert J. Dunlap typifies the tyrannical leader. Known as Chainsaw Al for his policies of wanton downsizing, Dunlap finally came to grief in his last position as chairman of the Sunbeam Corporation. After Dunlap ran up six months of losses (and raised doubts about the accuracy of corporate financial statements for the previous fiscal year), the board stepped in and fired him, and the Securities and Exchange Commission recently indicted him for financial improprieties.[11] Linda Wachner, former CEO of the now bankrupt apparel maker Warnaco, suffered a similar fate. Her acerbic and brash style alienated many investors, who are now suing her for concealing Warnaco's precarious financial condition. Harold Geneen, CEO of IT&T in the 1960s, was another autocratic leader who succeeded in retaining his managers only by grossly overpaying them.

Autocratic leaders often decide (or rationalize) that followers prefer not to be involved in the governance of the

---

11 Dunlap and other former executives of Sunbeam recently agreed to pay $15 million to settle a stockholder suit accusing them of inflating stock prices.

12 The Grand Inquisitor of Russian novelist Fyodor Dostoevsky, *The Brothers Karamazov* is such a leader.

institution.[12] Some other autocrats assume that the followers are too ignorant or helpless to know how to behave; the paternalistic CEO found in many old-line corporations represents this type of leader.[13]

Leaders who adapt an autocratic style, particularly in contemporary society, tend to have short tenures. Effective leaders must always engage the collective aspirations of the followers.

The reactive leader

Our second archetype is the reactive leader, the puppet or marionette controlled by his followers. The energy in this model flows upward from the followers to the leader.

An accident of corporate or political history often thrusts reactive leaders into their positions. Lacking purpose or vision of their own, they allow the tide of history to carry them along. Often such leaders feel unworthy of the mantle they have inherited. Consequently, a typical strategy for reactive leaders is to cede to their followers the responsibility for setting direction. This is a familiar phenomenon in fraternal organizations and professional societies, and in firms in which distribution drives success (many property- and life-insurance companies). Other examples of reactive leadership include the United Nations and the International Olympic Committee. Leadership in these organizations has been relatively ineffective because the interests of the membership are misaligned on so many issues.

A more positive example of this leadership model is Mondragon, the Basque industrial cooperative. Founded in 1956 by a young priest, José María Arizmendiarrieta, to make oil cooking stoves and paraffin heaters, Mondragon is now the 7th largest company in Spain, with 60,000 employees and revenues in excess of $8 billion euros. The enterprise

---

13 The shepherd in *Plato's Republic*, carefully tending his flock of sheep, is an apt metaphor.

comprises over 150 companies, including manufacturers, service firms, research centers, and schools.

In a pluralistic society, leaders often conspire with followers to avoid leading. In these circumstances, leaders become no more than managers, coordinating a set of initiatives established by others. Woodrow Wilson pointed out cynically at the end of the nineteenth century that our political system was devised to prevent "responsible leadership," referring to the innumerable checks and balances on a president's actions.[14] Leaders in a democracy must seek popular approval if they are to extend their tenure in office. Former U.S. President Bill Clinton struggles to manage by consensus suggest this situation.[15]

There is, to be sure, a subtle and important difference between a reactive leader and a responsive servant leader, a model portrayed in German novelist Hermann Hesse's *Journey to the East*.[16] In this novella, he describes the activities of Leo, the factotum who attends carefully to the needs of a group of travelers. The travelers begin to appreciate his contributions only after he mysteriously disappears one day. Many years later, they discover him to be the revered head of an important religious society. The moral of Hesse's tale, of course, is that followers will respond freely only to individuals who are chosen as leaders because they have cultivated trust in a role as servants of the people.

The participative leader

In this paragon of leadership style, the leader and the followers collaborate, the result of recognition that they are part of an interdependent system; their destiny is codetermined. Energy and information flow both down from the leader to the

---

14 Address to the Virginia Bar Association, August 4, 1898.
15 The ill-conceived national healthcare initiative, spearheaded by Hillary Clinton, illustrates the perils of attempting to satisfy all the stakeholders in a situation.
16 Robert K. Greenleaf elaborates on this model in *Servant Leadership* (Paulist Press, 1971), as does Max DePree in his *Leadership is an Art*, Dell, 1989.

followers and up from the followers to the leader. If a leader aligns with the followers, positive feedback amplifies the signals. Since power is distributed in this model, followers are empowered to act in ways that are consistent with the values and purpose of the organization.

The ideal model for participative leader was propounded in the 6th century B.C. by the great Taoist sage Lao Tzu. In his Tao Te Ching, we find the image of a self-effacing leader—who is effective despite his low profile:[17]

> *When the Master governs, the people are*
> *Hardly aware that he exists.*
> *Next best is a leader who is loved.*
> *Next one who is feared.*
> *The worst is one who is despised.*
> *If you don't trust the people,*
> *You make them untrustworthy.*
> *The Master doesn't talk, he acts.*

In a participative system, followers will have as much influence on the leader as do leaders on the followers, for the leader cannot maintain authority and power unless the followers believe in the cause. Followers cannot abdicate responsibility and become sycophants or toadies—they must join with the leader in a communal effort in which both leader and followers act to advance the higher needs of the enterprise. Leaders and followers in these circumstances have a covenant or social contract, one that is different from a shared madness or *folie à deux*, which allows uncritical mutual acceptance of goals and behavior. The covenant includes the responsibility of followers to give strong and fearless feedback to leaders. It was the Microsoft techies who convinced Bill Gates at Microsoft to reconsider his dismissal of the Internet as a "passing fad" and commit the firm to an aggressive Internet strategy.

17 See the excellent Steven Mitchell translation of the *Tao Te Ching*, Harper Perennial, 1991 (especially Chapters 17 and 57), or the recent translation by Ursula K. LeGuin, *Lao Tzu, Tao Te Ching*, Shambala, 1997.

A formation of Canadian geese in flight (Exhibit 6-1) provides a strong metaphor for the relationship between leaders and followers in a community:[18]

> ➢ Organization. The "V" formation provides drafting for each bird behind the lead bird. The cumulative lift can increase the range of the formation by as much as 71 percent.
> ➢ Alignment. Birds who leave the formation encounter significant drag and turbulence. This serves as a powerful reminder of the energy and power of the group.
> ➢ Leadership roles. The bird in front breaks new space and therefore expends more energy. As he tires, the other geese rotate in and out of the front position. They share leadership.
> ➢ Teamwork. Several comrades accompany a wounded or sick goose when it is forced to land, staying with it until it recovers or dies. The survivors catch up with the flock or find a new formation to join.

Organizations having effective leaders are always populated by effective followers. Some followers are pitiful and self-pitying Dilberts. Some revolt when they fail to embrace a leader's vision. Good followers challenge a leader to do better—they recognize that leaders and followers comprise a symbiotic system. Inept followers impair the efficacy of leaders, however capable they may appear to be. The most brilliant visionary will inevitably fail if his or her followers do not support the vision. Such leaders are like silver-tongued orators who never win an election (for example, Henry Clay and Adlai Stevenson.)

Leaders reveal confidence in their followers when they freely delegate and empower.

For example, at Southwest Airlines, by most standards the most successful airline of the past twenty years, CEO

---

18 Speech by Angeles Arrien, 1991.

6.1 | LEADERS AND FOLLOWERS IN FLIGHT

Herb Kelleher exhorted the members of his team to "Do what you feel like doing for the customer." Jan Carlson, the former Chairman of SAS (Scandinavian Airline), established similar policy guidelines for dealing with customers. He pointed out that the behavior of attendants and flight crews during the first 15 seconds of the encounter with customers—the "moment of truth"—determined the customer's impression of the company. The Ritz-Carlton Hotels have successfully created the same customer-centric culture.

Any leaders who attempt to address the needs of the community may risk becoming the beneficiary of the projections of the followers, who position them as heroes (in good time) or scapegoats (in bad times). Such transference or neurotic codependency is common when leaders try to satisfy mythic expectations.[19] Witness the Wizard of Oz, who

19 See Manfred F.R. deVries, *The Irrational Executive*, International Universities Press, 1984.

masqueraded as a powerful potentate until Dorothy and her friends discovered him to be an ordinary man.

Leaderless groups

The ultimate realization of the Taoist leadership model is the *leaderless group*, which can only emerge when the members of a community share values and have clarity about their direction. Such a leaderless group compensates for the absence of a formal leader through a process of self-alignment.[20] String quartets and small jazz ensembles, for example, lack obvious leaders—yet they may create exceptional music.[21] Communication within these small groups is continuous; always aural, of course, but also by gesture and expression. This becomes especially important when the players begin to introduce the uncertainty of improvisation.

In the absence of a formal leader, groups will be effective if they share these three attributes:

- They have mutual understanding. Its members all grasp exactly the goals of the activity or project, and they share in the quest for excellence. Strong external direction is unnecessary if the players are clear about the name of the game.
- They are competent. Each trusts the other to perform his or her part, knowing that each player is necessary to the success of the group.
- They have a mechanism for communicating. Quick

---

20 The phenomenon of magnetism is a relevant metaphor. When a magnetic field (force of the leader's vision) is applied to an unmagnetized bar of iron, the randomly oriented domains in the iron (the followers) realign themselves in the direction of the flux. The realignment may be delayed; this delay (the lag between cause and effect) is termed hysteresis.

21 See the example of the Portland String Quartet by Christian F. Poulson II and Stanley C Abraham, "The Portland String Quartet," *Journal of Management Inquiry*, September 1966.

feedback allows each player to sense a perturbation and become part of the solution. Members are willing to accept and act on constructive criticism.

In leaderless groups, individuals share the role of the leader as they submerge their identities in the greater purpose of the group. But they preserve their individuality to the extent that each person is empowered to make responsible decisions. And the group in fact does act as if there were a leader, despite the absence of any single person who plays this role—virtual leadership ensues. Leadership is both joint and rotating, depending on the need for given skills or insights at the moment. An Amish barn-raising is an example of this process.

A community of practice is similar. These informal groups bond together around a common theme, interest, or mission. They collaborate directly, develop their own culture, and yet do not appear on any organization chart. Communes and co-ops are examples of such practice communities.

Can this model of leaderless groups be applied to large numbers of people? Only up to a point, for complete alignment of the individual members of the group is difficult, and spatial separation allows entropy to increase, producing potential instability. This suggests that, unless we install rigorous controls, we can set an upper limit on the effective size of any organizational unit. Some theorists propose that performance begins to falter when the unit size exceeds 150 persons. The errant behavior of employees in firms such as Metropolitan Life (deceptive sales practices) and General Electric (falsification of accounting records) may be a symptom of this condition. In pragmatic terms, if the organization is too large, good government becomes more difficult; if too small, it may not have the resources to sustain itself.

The role of power and authority

Power and authority are important leadership assets, for they enable the leader to influence the organization. History has shown that without power there can be no real change, yet too much power corrupts a leader. Unless it is guided by reason and purpose, power is arbitrary and feckless. How, asks James MacGregor Burns "can we subdue the voracious, crafty, and inescapable beast of power?"[22] One answer is to protect man's rights, as in the Magna Carta, signed by King John of England in 1215, or to set up a system of checks and balances, as in the U.S. federal government's equilibrium between the legislative, executive, and judicial branches. But all leaders need to heed Lord Acton's famous caution: "Power tends to corrupt, and absolute power corrupts absolutely."[23]

The power of a leader stems from several sources. Wealth and fame represent common sources of power, as does charisma or a strong, magnetic personality. An expert derives power from his or her specialized knowledge. An elected or appointed official derives power from legitimate position. Power can stem from a leader's ability to reward or coerce, but the most effective source of power is the trust placed with the leader by the follower.

Sociologist Max Weber proposed that leadership evolved through three stages of authority: the Charismatic Stage (Christ and Mohammed as examples), the Rational/Legal Stage, and finally the Traditional Stage, in which we find legitimate organizations.[24] Weber defines charisma as the quality of an individual's personality by virtue of which he or she is set aside from ordinary men and treated as endowed with supernatural, superhuman, or at least exceptional powers

22 James MacGregor Burns, opus citus.
23 John Emerich Edward Dalberg, Baron Acton, April 3, 1887. Less known is the balance of Acton's statement: "Great men are almost always bad men."
24 Max Weber in H.H. Gerth and C. Wright Mills, *From Max Weber*, Oxford University Press, 1958.

and qualities. It is because of these qualities, Weber argues, that people come to be treated as leaders. In earlier times, people accorded this deference to prophets, healers, and to leaders in war or the hunt.

Good participative leaders may have little or no charisma, although it's hard to find any leader who does not exude an aura of confidence and commitment. But mere charisma does not engender true leadership, and charismatic individuals often fail the test of a good leader. Like Adolph Hitler or Joseph Stalin or Osama Bin Laden they may lack moral stature; their excesses of power can easily lead to atrocity. Or like Newt Gingrich or Ross Perot they are unable to express a cogent vision and a set of shared goals consonant with the values of the society they represent. Charismatic leaders may survive temporarily on the basis of their public persona and needs of their followers. Nevertheless, in the long run, character counts, and a strong personality is no substitute, as witness Richard Nixon's eventual demise as U.S. President when he breached the public trust.

One contemporary model explains charismatic leadership as the result of the complementary needs of leaders and followers.[25] The specific enabling conditions include a leader who achieves control and obedience from dependent followers who identify with the leader. In transactional leadership, leaders achieve compliance from independent followers by imposing rewards or punishments. In transforming leadership, by contrast, internalized shared values guide empowered leaders and empowered followers.

Organizations often confer authority on individuals in the expectation that they will render certain services. The authority may be formal, the result of rank or position, or it may be informal, based on trust, competence, or knowledge. Authority properly utilized may facilitate leadership, but it will not suffice to establish an individual as a leader. At best it allows leaders to get the attention of followers. Heads of

---

25 Marshall Sashkin, "Development of the Power Motive in Leaders and Follow-ers," A.K. Rice 12th Scientific Meeting, May 7, 1995.

organizations often inherit their followers; leaders need to earn the fealty, respect, and trust of their subordinates. Leaders who have no formal recognition as leaders and no authority must lead indirectly.

We can cite many powerful leaders who lacked authority. Neither Martin Luther King Jr. nor Mahatma Gandhi held any appointed or elected position. Yet, writing from his prison cell in Birmingham, Alabama, King exerted tremendous authority over three constituencies: the SCLC (Southern Christian Leadership Conference), a civil rights organization comprised primarily of African-American clergy; his admirers and followers; and the public at large. Gandhi's espousal of *satyagraha* (power of truth) was the foundation for his influence without authority. In 1930, he called on his followers to oppose the tax on salt that the British had imposed and organized a peaceful march to the sea to make salt by evaporating seawater. By exercising non-violent resistance, he empowered people ultimately to oust the British from India.

The handicap of hidden agendas

Leaders need to be sensitive to several conditions that may inhibit or compromise their attempts to achieve community. To begin with, hidden agendas may exist that detract from the community's overt agenda. Every group, according to psychologist Wilfred Bion, has both an overt agenda—the task that needs to be carried out—and a hidden agenda that exists at a deeper, latent level.[26] These hidden agendas conspire to create a basic assumption group (BAG). The work group seeks to complete one or more explicit tasks. In contrast, the BAG focuses inwardly on the members' wishes, fears, and fantasies. Bion identifies these four distinct BAGs:

26 Wilfrid R. Bion, "Experiences in Groups" *Group Relations Reader*, GREX, 1975.

Dependency. This group's hidden agenda is to derive security and protection from the leader. The group may behave with stupidity and ineptness in the hope that the leader will deliver them from their plight. If the leader fails (as he or she inevitably must), the group becomes hostile and deposes the leader.

Fight or Flight. The hidden agenda of this group is to survive by either fighting or fleeing from the task. Leaders of groups concerned with flight usually minimize the importance of the task.

Pairing. For individuals in this BAG, the hidden agenda is to bond together to provide intellectual or emotional support to one another. The group fantasizes that a savior will be born to help the group complete its task.

Oneness. In this hidden agenda, the members of the group seek union with a powerful external force or cause outside the group as a path to survival.

Since a group never exhausts its basic assumption, leaders may choose consciously to use the primal forces that generate the assumption. Most churches, for example, build upon the dependency assumption. Military and business organizations often motivate their members via the fight assumption.

Overcoming self-interest

A second obstacle to building a community may arise from the temptation for members of the community to act in their own self-interest. Leaders then face the challenge reconciling such self-interest with the greater needs of the community. Economist Adam Smith introduced the notion that an individual who tends only to his own gain will also promote the public interest.[27] He believed that they would be led, as if by an invisible hand, to achieve the best good for all. But in many situations this appears not to be the case, for individuals reaching rational decisions based on self-interest unwittingly conspire to damage the welfare of the system.

27 Adam Smith, *The Wealth of Nations*, 1776.

The historic depredation of the village commons reflects this seductive dynamic. The commons in 18th century England was a pasture open for grazing to all the livestock owned by the members of the village. The sharing system worked for centuries, because the pasture could support as many sheep as the villagers owned. But eventually a villager asks himself, "Why not add one more sheep to my herd?" He reasons that he will receive all the benefit, while the village as a whole must share the consequences of overgrazing. Each villager reasons similarly and thus commits to a strategy that compels him to increase his herd without limit—in a world that is limited. "Ruin is the destination towards which all men rush, each pursuing his own best interest in a society that believes in the freedom of the commons. Freedom in a commons brings ruin to all."[28]

We can view a more recent example of this phenomenon in the Big Bend area of Texas. Ranchers devastated the once-verdant grasslands around the Chisos Mountains after the State of Texas granted them free grazing privileges in 1942. Having nothing to lose, the ranchers increased their herds by a factor of five or six—and the last blade of grass soon disappeared. Re-vegetation began only after the National Park was established in 1944, although even today, six decades later, the recovery is far from complete.

For any leader, this illustrates the infamous "free rider" quandary—what to do, for example, with the passenger who rides the subway without paying, on the grounds that one more free ride will not make a difference. Or the individual who adds a little more pollution to the atmosphere, or continues to fish for endangered species, or picks the fragile wildflower along the alpine trail. Free riders take all the benefit but provide nothing in return.

In contemporary game theory, the tragedy of the commons appears as the "Prisoner's Dilemma," first formulated in 1950 by consultant Albert Tucker. Guards isolate two partners in crime, offering each reduced sentences if they

28 Garrett Hardin, "The Tragedy of the Commons," *Science*, 162, 1968.

will turn state's evidence and implicate their partner. If both inform, they each serve two years. If neither informs, they each serve one year. If only one informs, the guards set him free, while his partner gets a three-year sentence. Rational self-interest supports a strategy of "inform", for the sentence will be either two years or freedom; failure to inform will yield a sentence of either three years or one year. And yet if both prisoners endorse this logic, they maximize their combined served time (four years).

The Prisoner's Dilemma is a specialized case of the more general two-person, non-cooperative, non-zero-sum game. Mathematician John F. Nash demonstrated in 1950 that all such games have a rational solution (the Nash equilibrium). But in the troublesome Prisoner's Dilemma, a better outcome is achieved by apparently non-rational behavior, and leaders need to formulate policies to address this paradox.

In the corporate world, the analog of inform/do not inform is compete/collaborate. Logic again appears to support the compete option. Yet, as in the Prisoner's Dilemma, a better outcome ensues when both parties cooperate—most obviously when transactions must be repeated.

Game theorist Robert Axelrod's computer simulation, in fact, shows that a Tit-for-Tat strategy works best in the long run, because the shadow of future outcomes falls heavily on today's decisions.[29] In this strategy, a player cooperates so long as his opponent does, but retaliates immediately if the other player fails to cooperate. The complete tactical plan for Tit-for-Tat is the following:

1) Be nice (do not defect first) and be forgiving.
2) Reciprocate immediately; be provocable.
3) Do not be envious. In a non-zero-sum game, you do not have to do better than the others to do well yourself, particularly in a game with many players. For example, a successful relationship with a supplier entails that both you and the supplier be profitable. If

---

29 Robert Axelrod, *The Evolution of Cooperation*, Basic Books, 1984.

you try to reduce the supplier's profit by not paying his or her bills, he or she will ultimately retaliate by reducing service or quality—or not delivering at all! The right strategy in a cooperative world requires that you both do well.

4) Do not be too clever. Negotiating strategies that are random or devious or too complex will confuse the other party, who may then conclude that you are unresponsive to his or her needs.

Leaders may be tempted to eschew collaboration in the case of a single private transaction. But if they must engage in repeated transactions, collaboration pays off. And even when only a single transaction takes place, their reputations will pursue them into the future

A similar dilemma occurs when many individuals attempt to work together. They have the option of being noble (cooperating) or selfish (not cooperating). If they act nobly, they help others at their own expense. If they are selfish, they help themselves at others' expense. In this latter case, if their behavior is public, it damages their reputations, and they may suffer long-term consequences. On the village commons, everyone knows—they need only count the herd. But what if decisions and behaviors are private, i.e., if no one knows what decisions have been made?

In the long run, a strategy of alliance with other organizations can pay rich dividends to all of the partners. Sociobiologist Robert Wright makes a compelling case for nonzero-sum behavior as the critical component of cultural and economic evolution.[30]

Leaders face major challenges in building a culture that values collaboration and nonzero-sum behavior. After all, English philosopher Thomas Hobbes contended that selfish people competing against one another would always dominate society; a strong government, in Hobbes view, represented

---

30 Robert Wright, *Nonzero*, Vintage Books, 2001.

the only safeguard against mutual self-destruction.[31] Rousseau countered with the contention that man's intrinsic compassion would overrule greed if private property were abolished, an argument later adopted with considerable force by German political philosopher Karl Marx in his *Communist Manifesto*.

The evidence on a global scale surely confirms that cooperative policies are hard to sustain in a non-cooperative environment. And how can any society resist invasion by predators and free riders? Every leader and his or her followers face exactly this quandary. How can leaders construct a value system in which individuals behave for the mutual benefit of all of its members, honoring the implicit social contract? How can leaders create a culture of cooperation, in lieu of the privatization solution where all solve their own problems?

The leader who seeks to create a community when each of its members faces the free rider temptation has several strategies beyond the classic approach of enforcement prescribed by Hobbes or the reversion to privatization. His or her first option is to change the rules, for instance, adjusting the compensation system to reward group initiative, thus penalizing (or at least giving less credit to) individual initiatives. The best option for leaders, however, is to educate the members of the organization, changing their values and behavior, and eventually establishing a setting where people *want* to do the right thing. Beneficent leaders find that culture does matter—communicating mission and values will have a measurable and positive impact on performance.

The illusion of invulnerability

Leaders invariably find that a strong community, one in which values, beliefs, attitudes, and behaviors are congruent, tends to perform exceptionally well. Everyone focuses on the same goals and executes the organization's strategies with efficiency. Later in the life of such a community, however, its members tend to adopt the illusion of invulnerability.

31 Thomas Hobbes, *Leviathan*, 1651.

This is the third pitfall that the beneficent leader must overcome. The sharp focus and narrow outlook of high performers make them reluctant to consider alternatives to the status quo when threats appear on the horizon.[32] After all, their strategies have produced growth and more success. But this very growth and success forces them to install more internal systems and procedures. The focus of the firm then shifts from the external customer to the internal customer. The arrogant and self-reflexive culture that often ensues has a powerful inherent resistance to change. We saw good examples of this phenomenon in the 1970s and 1980s at IBM and Digital Equipment in the computer industry and at Ford and General Motors in the automobile industry. The parable of *The Crocodile in the Bedroom* is instructive (Exhibit 6-2).

One of the leader's strategies for overcoming this self-centeredness (and the associated complacency) is to introduce diversity and disorder. Most organizations can support a small subculture that espouses different values or behavior patterns. These subcultures can sometimes disrupt operations in the rest of the firm. Consequently, when management has scarce resources or wants to maximize efficiency, it often acts to suppress or oust the rebels.

Yet, as we have seen throughout history, even monarchs need at least one fool or rebel to keep them sane. Professional fools, revered as tellers of truth, flourished from the time of the Egyptian Pharaohs until well into the eighteenth century. Imperial Romans engaged household jesters, and fools were common during the Renaissance in courts, taverns, and brothels. In *King Lear*, Shakespeare's play of fallen majesty, the fool is a strangely wise companion who, as he travels with the broken old king, comments acerbically on the behavior of humankind.

Innovation will flourish when a leader introduces the appropriate amount of diversity and entropy. Too much order

---

32 The alligator and some mammals possess a third eyelid, the nictitating membrane. This eyelid protects them, but it also prevents them from seeing—like managers who think they have no choices.

6.2 | THE CROCODILE IN THE BEDROOM

A crocodile became increasingly fond of the wallpaper in his bedroom. He stared at it for hours and hours. "Just look at all those neat and tidy rows of flowers and leaves," said the Crocodile. "They are like soldiers. There is not a single one that is out of place."

"My dear," said the Crocodile's wife, "you are spending too much time in bed. Come out into my garden where the air is fresh and the sun is bright and warm."

"Well if you insist, for just a few minutes," said the Crocodile. He put on a pair of dark sunglasses to protect his eyes from the glare and went outside.

Mrs. Crocodile was proud of her garden. "Look at all the hollyhocks and marigolds," she said. "Smell the roses and lilies of the valley."

"Great heavens!" cried the Crocodile, "The flowers and leaves in this garden are growing in a terrible tangle! They are all scattered. They are messy and entwined!"

The Crocodile rushed back into his bedroom in a state of great distress. He was at once comforted by the sight of his wallpaper. "Ah," said the Crocodile. "Here is a garden that is ever so much better. How happy and secure these flowers make me feel."

After that the Crocodile seldom left his bed. He lay there, smiling at the walls. He turned a pale and sickly shade of green.

Without a doubt, there is such a thing as too much order.

Arnold Lobell, *Fables*, Harper, 1980
Artwork courtesy of Mary Jane Begin

engenders bureaucracy, stifling the creativity of a group and driving it toward stagnation.[33] Most U.S. corporations, unfortunately, have this strong Confucian bias, for they consider chaos to be the enemy of efficiency; they value hierarchy and a highly ordered state. Excessive structure, if coupled

33 David S. Landes argues persuasively that the persistent elevation of authority in many Islamic and Roman Catholic countries has cramped initiative and encouraged values inimical to experimentation. *The Wealth and Poverty of Nations*, W.W.Norton & Co., 1998.

with the draconian constraints of bureaucracy, will force innovative individuals to flee the enterprise.[34]

Too much disorder and entropy, on the other hand, allows so much disarray that the firm loses its way no less surely than if it foundered on the shoals of bureaucracy; pure novelty, adopted for its own sake, will generate only chaos.

Leaders can honor disorder within the units or subdivisions of the organization if the organization as a whole has unity and clarity of purpose; constructive dissension and conflict will energize any organization. Disorder is the breeding ground for creativity, and good leaders prosper by "letting a hundred flowers blossom and a hundred schools of thought contend."[35] Good leaders apply these insights and allow sufficient disorder (novelty) within the organization so that innovation (practical inventions) can flourish. They introduce "genetic diversity" within the organization to help promote this innovation.

This philosophy accounts for 3M's historic success in producing a continuing stream of new products; management allows employees to devote a portion of their time at work to unplanned projects.[36] An effective leader introduces just enough disorder to nurture the innate creativity of the firm. As illustrated in Exhibit 6-3, innovation is optimized when enough complexity is sustained to allow diversity to flourish, without destabilizing the enterprise.

Most bold new ideas are foolish; they are more likely to lead the organization astray than to transform it. The task for leaders (and their followers), then, is to distinguish the heretics who show us the path to an exciting new place from the

---

34 Some rules, however, can stimulate creativity. Poets have composed thousands of brilliant verses within the strict boundaries of the haiku, a seventeen-syllable Japanese form. Shakespeare disarms us with his love sonnets that adhere to a fourteen-line structure.

35 Chairman Mao speech on May 2, 1956. The Chairman's words were, unfortunately, louder than his actions.

36 Although Lew Lehr, 3M's former Chairman, ruefully observed that, "Most of the real entrepreneurs have long left our corporation."

6.3 | OPTIMIZING CREATIVITY

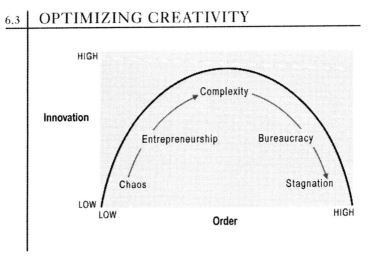

psychotics who will bring disaster upon us if we follow them. Leaders must sort out the potential geniuses of their organizations from those who hallucinate at the lunatic fringe, for sometimes such heretics are destructive.

Nevertheless, as a result of their visionary impulses, leaders feel empowered to take risks that others dare not take.[37] This suggests that greatness is associated with iconoclasm, a quality that conflicts with the need of the organization for safe and reliable behavior. After all, many Europeans were confident that the earth was flat until Columbus completed his historic expedition in 1492. Imagine, as a leader, you found these eccentrics in your organization:

> ➤ Nicolau Copernicus. This Polish astronomer boldly proclaimed in 1530 that man was no longer the center of the universe, but that the earth revolved around the sun! Scientists and theologians had accepted Ptolemy's premise that the sun revolved

37 After the Wright Brothers historic manned-airplane flight (120 feet in 12 seconds) in Kitty Hawk, North Carolina on December 17, 1903, Orville declared, "I looked back with amazement at the audacity of our attempt."

around the earth since the second century. Copernicus became a pariah for his unorthodox views.

➢ Leonardo da Vinci. This Renaissance scientist and artist was a creative genius. But da Vinci was dead wrong in many of his boldest speculations; he sketched helicopters, ornithopters, and assorted other ingenious machines that could not fly.

➢ Charles Darwin. Darwin postulated that man was part of the animal kingdom, and that evolution occurred by natural selection. His claims generated violent controversy, some of which persists to this day.

Leaders always have hard decisions to make when a new paradigm, a challenge to corporate policy, presents itself. Greek playwright Sophocles describes the conflict between Antigone and Creon in his classic play *Antigone*.[38] At the battle of Thebes, the two brothers Polyneices and Eteocles, who vie for rulership of the city, kill one another. Creon, taking over as king, decrees that Polyneices, who had attacked the city, shall remain unburied. Antigone, sister of the two brothers, defies her uncle Creon by giving Polyneices a token burial. Although Antigone is engaged to Haimon, Creon's son, Creon condemns her to be buried alive for her defiance of his edict. As the tragedy unfolds, both Antigone and Haimon commit suicide, and Eurydice, Haimon's mother, also kills herself.

Sopohocles' play illustrates for us the conflict between the rights of the individual and the rights of the state. Creon's principle is obedience to power in order to assure the stability of the state. "Nations belong to men with power," he announces. To his courtiers, he says "One who cherishes an individual beyond his homeland, he, I say, is nothing." And later, speaking to Haimon, "If I rear a dissident family, I am feeding general disorder. The state, when she sets someone

---

38 Sophocles, *Antigone*, translated by Richard Emil Braun, Oxford University Press, 1973.

up, you must obey him." Antigone's individualism, her resistance to the pressure to conform, has a familial motive. But she criticizes Creon for his attempt to "violate the lawful traditions," that is, the laws made for man by the Gods. Creon acts like a leader. But he achieves a zero-sum outcome—his gain is Antigone's loss.[39] A truly effective leader seeks win-win results.

The merits of Creon's case aside, *Antigone* presents for leaders a common conundrum: whether to follow the will of the people or do what the leader believes to be right. Pragmatic politicians cannot squander their power and goodwill on every just cause. But men do not become great leaders because of their ability to compromise; they must often persist in the face of public opposition. Woodrow Wilson describes the consequences: "Friends desert and despise them. They stand alone, and oftentimes are made bitter by their isolation. They are doing nothing less than defy human opinion."[40]

In society as a whole, a collective tyranny stifles eccentricity, and even custom or hallowed tradition can become despotic. As British philosopher John Stuart Mill has observed, man needs protection against the oppression of prevailing opinion and feeling, against the tendency of society to impose its own ideas as rules of conduct.[41] Majority opinion, as we know, may produce mediocre outcomes. The moral is clear: leaders must be true to their own values and sense of what is right, regardless of the consequences. Compromise may be necessary in the short term but, in the long run, is not an acceptable option for great leaders.

It is no surprise that leaders must contend with conflict as they attempt to change and deal with individual agendas. This

39 In a zero-sum situation, the total benefits are fixed; gain by one participant must come at the expense of the other participants. In nonzero-sum situations, the behavior of the participants may increase the total benefits.
40 Woodrow Wilson, "Leaders of Men, an Address," 1890.
41 John Stuart Mill, *On Liberty*, 1859.

entails that leaders master the art of negotiation. The various negotiation strategies include *avoidance* (ignoring the issues), *accommodating* (yielding one's position), *competing* (acting as if the transaction had a zero-sum outcome), and *compromising* (half for me, half for you). Effective leaders, however, attempt to reach agreements by *collaborating* to achieve non-zero-sum outcomes (win-win results).[42] In an economic world that we can view as a large set of two-person games, coalitions may provide considerable benefits, although negotiating the division of these benefits can be a challenge. (See the Coalition Game in Appendix 6-5)

Every leader, of course, inherits diversity in his or her organization. Various individuals have differing degrees of competence and commitment. One of the leader's tasks is to instill an ethic that says: "we can all evolve to a higher level," and the leader's charge is to provide vehicles for personal development and learning for followers at all levels.

The effective leader, in other words, attends to the needs of the organization—for economic stability, social responsibility, and ethical behavior.

Can we also hold the leader responsible for the needs of the individuals who comprise the organization? How, indeed, can the leader even know what their needs are? In a highly evolved enterprise, every individual senses his or her role and responds intuitively to the overall needs of the situation. Those just entering a community (like minor-league players advancing to the majors) may need explicit directions. The leader must then function as a coach, a mentor, a teacher. The leader's role then becomes tacit, as in Lao Tzu's paragon of Taoist leadership.

Dealing with incompetents presents a particular dilemma. Are they to be fired or nurtured? GE's former chairman Jack Welch recommends that management dismiss the lower-performing ten percent of the organization each year. This

---

42 The reader will find good presentations of this philosophy in the writings of Roger Fisher and William Ury. For example, see *Getting to Yes*, Penguin Books, 1991.

view of extreme meritocracy seems to lead inevitably to internal competition and a degradation of any sense of community within the organization—a rejection of loyalty as an important corporate value!

Another dilemma is the pressure to downsize, regardless of competence. This has become a popular tactic for corporations in the past year as they respond to low cost and efficiency as critical survival factors. Many firms during the period 1999-2002 dismissed up to 30% of their work force. And indeed economic theory endorses downsizing by arguing that the smaller firm will remain viable, while displaced workers go on to productive jobs elsewhere.

Leaders and followers share the responsibility, however, for maintaining job security. On the one hand, leaders must plan with sufficient foresight to obviate the need for abrupt reductions in staff. They must support continuous growth and learning, so that employees acquire the skills to find work elsewhere. Leaders who suddenly become aware of the need for efficiency have not met this criterion. (Some CEOs cut head count to make themselves look good in a hurry!) At the same time, all the members of the community share responsibility for their own destiny, for maintaining "employability." They must acquire the skills necessary to cope with adversity and adapt to changing circumstances.

Building a community

How can leaders build a community and a culture in which people embrace the same values and vision and behave in ways that are consistent with these values? Building a community is an undertaking that cannot be completed in a day or a month—it may take years to develop such a community and culture. The action plan for the leader who has this goal is threefold:

1) Articulating a clear statement of values and purpose

and sharing an inspiring vision to which people can commit with enthusiasm.

2) Acting as a role model for the community. Leaders nurture a sense of community by

> *Who they are.* Effective leaders embody integrity, passion, empathy, and similar leadership virtues.

> *What they do.* Leaders behave in ways that promote learning and empowerment. Effective leaders reward appropriate behavior and penalize inappropriate behavior.

> *What they say.* They tell stories about the past, present, and future. Leadership does not imply giving answers. On the contrary, leaders inspire the community to find its own answers, mobilizing people to solve problems.

Effective communication starts with listening to the voices of the followers. Only then can the leader focus on outward communication, both verbal and non-verbal. Leaders relate to the community by celebrating the past, sharing stories about what happened yesterday: the history of the organization, how it started, where it has been, the journeys it has taken, and the tragedies and triumphs of the past. Effective leaders create a mythology and a set of traditions to support the group on its current journey.

No less important are the stories that leaders tell about today. Individuals can only live out their lives from moment to moment. What's happening now is the only reality— the past is irretrievable and the future is unknowable. To quote Czech President

Havel Václav "We live in the post-modern world, where anything is possible and almost nothing is certain." Enhancing our awareness of these moment-to-moment events, concentrating on those that are important and putting energy into them—this is the pattern that leaders reinforce.

The third element in the leader's communications portfolio consists of visionary stories about tomorrow. This is where the leader tells us about Camelot, Shangri-La, the Big Rock Candy Mountain. We find hope and inspiration in these stories, and we are reminded that our labors will be rewarded. Words are a primary source of power for leaders, both for what they say and for what they fail to say.

The greatest leaders are consummate raconteurs. Their stories about the past describe where we came from, what we accomplished, our heroes and heroines. Their stories about the present describe where we are, who we are, what is important to us. Their stories about an exciting future give us a vision of where we must go and how we will get there, the obstacles to be overcome and the rewards to be gained. Followers eventually look behind the leader's words, of course, to see if behavior fits speech. As a result, leaders must not only tell their own stories, they must embody the stories they tell. As a role model, the leader must act in ways that preserve the community. As Gandhi eloquently observed, "My life is its own message."

3) Providing opportunities to share information and experience. Trust grows when individuals have the

opportunity to interact, to share ideas and perceptions, and to work and play together. We often disparage play as a builder of community, but it is during play that we see our colleagues at their most authentic.

Shakespeare's Henry V calls upon this tactic before leading his men into battle against the French on St. Crispin's Day:

> *We few, we happy few, we band of brothers:*
> *For he today that sheds his blood with me*
> *Shall be my brother; be he ne'er so vile*
> *This day shall gentle his condition;*
> *And gentlemen in England now abed*
> *Shall think themselves accursed they were not here*
> *And hold their manhoods cheap whiles any speaks*
> *That fought with us upon Saint Crispin's day.*[43]

Leaders make frequent use of ritual and symbol to reinforce the ethos of the community. Duke's Mike Krzyzewski, perhaps the most successful college basketball coach of this era, teaches his players the power of working as a team with the image of five fingers, representing communication, trust, collective responsibility, caring, and pride, all forming a clenched fist.[44]

Conclusion

In an ideal community, the alignment of a leader and his or her followers produces synergy, a compounding of energy. Followers and leader sense their roles and respond instinctively to the needs of the enterprise. The leader draws energy from the followers, like an actor from the audience or teacher from the students. Leaders catalyze, they behave in ways that enable the organization to realize more of its

---

43 William Shakespeare, *King Henry the Fifth*, Act 4, Scene 3.
44 *The New York Times*, March 25, 2001.

potential; they transform drones into effective follower-workers.

Creating a community is a crucial dimension of the leader's role that his or her style can either impede or facilitate. In my experience, a participative style is always the best choice for the leader. (Autocratic leadership, ironically, can produce a sense of community among those who resent or feel oppressed by such leaders.) The right style will reward the leader with greater power as followers place greater trust in the leader.

Even a powerful leader, however, needs to overcome the handicap of hidden agendas and the insidious effect of self-interest. And he or she must combat the common delusion of invulnerability by stressing the pervasiveness of change and the importance of considering diverse perspectives on the future.

The beneficent leader's program begins with clear values and purpose and follows with an inspired vision and strategy. The behavior of the leader can either undermine or reinforce the community. What he or she does and how he or she communicates are critical. Leaders tell inspiring stories about the future (although when the story is ended, it may be time for the leader to move on!)

For the beneficent leader, building a strong community is far more than an act of pure altruism. It has powerful pragmatic benefits for the leader, for strong community makes possible the implementation of strategies, programs, and projects. And it allows the enterprise and the *adaptive leader* to deal more effectively with the continuing challenge of change, the topic of our next chapter.

Appendix 6-A
The Coalition Game

Groups A, B, and C are three independent organizations. Each has designated a representative to send to a three-way negotiation. The representatives are empowered to commit their organizations. The three organizations have been told by a higher authority that if they work together they can realize significant benefits:

If A, B, and C can agree to work together, they can share benefits totaling $121 million. How they want to divide up the benefits is up to them, but they must agree on the exact allocation of benefits before they will be made available. If only two of the parties work together, there are lesser benefits available (schedule below).

Benefit Schedule

A alone	$0
B alone	$0
C alone	$0
A and B together	$118 million
A and C together	$84 million
B and C together	$5 million
A, B, and C together get	$121 million

Any pair that decides to work together must provide an explicit allocation benefit before the benefits are handed over. Only one agreement is possible. Either the parties agree to a three-way allocation or two of the parties agree to work together, leaving the third party with nothing. Each representative's goal is to get the maximum benefits.

Chapter 7

The Adaptive Leader

Better start swimming or you'll sink like a stone
For the times, they are a changing.
—Bob Dylan

Those who have become accomplished in their roles as purposeful, visionary, strategic, and beneficent leaders cannot rest on their laurels. They must also function as *adaptive leaders*, addressing the challenge of continuous change. In a heterogeneous global economy connected by the Internet, change is the rule, not the exception.[1] Yesterday's strategy may have been brilliant, even elegant. But the odds are that today or tomorrow a shift in the market, a competitor's new tactics, a technological innovation, a federal or local regulation will render it obsolete. Good leaders strive to be the first to understand change and to position the organization where it can withstand or even benefit from new conditions.

This is why good leaders don't expend all their energy to promote stasis. Their proper goal is to achieve dynamic equilibrium as the organization adjusts either to external variables—customer needs, competitor initiatives, or

---

1 The pervasiveness of change is not a new phenomenon. We can trace its discovery at least back to the Greek philosopher Heraclitus, who noted that "Upon those who step into the same rivers, different and ever different waters flow down." Impermanence is a central tenet of both Buddhism and Taoism, while the three aspects of Brahman in Hinduism include Brahman (the creator), Vishnu (the preserver), and Shiva (the destroyer).

economic, social, technological, and political trends—or to internal variables—the changing aspirations of individuals as a result of their development and maturation. To avoid slow decay, therefore, adaptive leaders must overcome many employees' natural preference for stability in lieu of change. Leaders must stimulate vitality and enthusiasm for the challenge of confronting change and the evolution of the organization through its lifecycle.[2]

Stage 1 of the organization's life cycle

The life cycle of the typical organization is shown in Exhibit 7-1. In Stage 1, management operates with a clear vision and dominant theme. The firm carries out a set of strategies that satisfies customers in a particular market segment, the firm's performance improves, and it prospers. Sooner or later, however, if the firm becomes insensitive to changing externalities, growth slows.

History's slow and sometimes imperceptible rates of change often lull leaders into believing that they are masters of their future, one which will be very much like the past. But the price they pay for living only in the past is to become part of history. Rapid access to global information today can produce sudden and drastic change. And when change materializes, it is rarely reversible. As a result, leaders must look hard and continuously for early warning signals, clues to what may become major discontinuities. Andrew Grove, former CEO of Intel, the world's leading manufacturer of microprocessors and integrated circuits, describes these as "10X events."[3] Examples of such momentous discontinuities include the Arab oil embargo of 1972, deregulation of the telecommunications industry in 1982, and the advent of the

---

2 Nietzsche refers to this attitude as *amor fati* (love of fate), the ability to accept whatever happens, whatever people do, with equanimity and enthusiasm.
3 Andrew S. Grove, *Only the Paranoid Survive*, Doubleday, 1996.

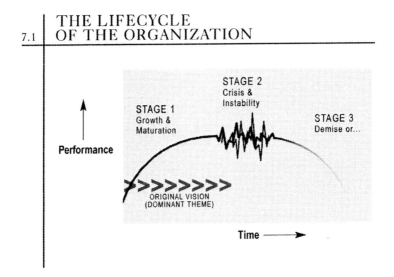

7.1 | THE LIFECYCLE OF THE ORGANIZATION

Internet in late 1960s (although its influence was not felt broadly until the 1990s).

The concept of a disruptive technology is similar.[4] These are technologies that may have little appeal to current customers, but have the potential to serve effectively the needs of future customers. Apple Computer, for example, led in the world of personal computing for a time, but lagged behind the leaders in bringing the laptop to the market.

Stage 2 of the organization's life cycle

Whether change comes from outside the enterprise or from within, eventually but inexorably, the organization enters Stage 2, a period of serious flux and instability. A crisis may arise in a few months, as in 2001 with Exodus Communications, a major provider of Internet hosting services, or only after many years, as has been the case with Burlington

---

4 Joseph L. Bower and Clayton M. Christensen, "Disruptive Technologies: Catching the Wave," *Harvard Business Review*, January-February 1995.

Industries, at one time America's largest textile manufacturer. Both of these one-time leaders recently declared bankruptcy.[5] The important point is that organizations cannot maintain themselves on the plateau of this trajectory—they must either grow or falter.

Often leaders react by exhorting their subordinates to work harder, or by applying rigorous cost controls, or by downsizing. The reality is that, if the vision and strategy of the enterprise have become irrelevant to the needs of the customer or to social, political, or environmental conditions, these corrective measures only serve to delay the inevitable.

The dominant theme or essential character of the firm often blurs at this point if the leaders decide to diversify in order to continue growth. But a painful demise in Stage 3 inevitably follows Stage 2, sometimes quickly, sometimes over a prolonged time period.

Stage 3 of the organization's life cycle

The life cycle of the organization in Stage 3 can evolve in one of two ways. For the leader who fails to adapt and refocus the organization, extinction is the outcome.

A number of factors may lead to this Stage 3 scenario, such as changes in government regulation, failure to recognize shifts in customer needs, and insensitivity to the environment. But the entry of aggressive new competitors with new technology is the most common threat to the status quo. Looked at through the lens of history, we can witness the impact of Joseph Schumpeter's creative destructionism: entrepreneurs destroy old economic systems and structures in order to create new ones.[6] This Austrian economist argued in 1942 that technological change "incessantly revolutionizes

---

5 Exodus Communications managed to realize losses during the first 9 months of 2001 of $4 billion on revenues of $900 million!

6 Joseph A. Schumpeter, *Capitalism, Socialism, and Democracy*, Harper & Bro., 1942.

the economic structure from within," and he viewed creative destruction as the source of human progress.

This rise and fall is not confined to the corporate community. Arnold Toynbee's monumental analysis of 21 civilizations showed that they all passed through a cycle of growth, maturity, and decline.[7] Leaders failed to prevent the disintegration of their realms by either "archaism" (a return to past behavior) or "futurism" (reaching out for some ideal future). Nor did hard work to fix the defects in the system avert the crisis. Toynbee suggests that "palingenesia"—total rebirth—is the only possible remedy.

In retrospect, we rarely find that crisis has materializes overnight—it germinates from conditions that begin to develop months or even years earlier. Efficiency and effectiveness begin to deteriorate, albeit slowly, as the relevance of the original dominant theme declines. Perspicacious leaders recognize this dynamic early and take steps to refocus the enterprise before instability sets in and decline becomes irreversible.

Slow adaptation may not be enough to cope with instability and the forces of change. In order to avoid the demise illustrated in Exhibit 7-1, sometimes the leader can launch the firm on an entirely different trajectory, illustrated in Exhibit 7-2. Such a renaissance or rebirth will demand that the old vision and dominant theme for the enterprise be replaced by new ones, sponsored by the head of the organization operating as a visionary leader.

This remedy often intimidates those who prospered in the old culture and values. As a consequence, salvation must come from leadership that is prepared to develop and adopt a new dominant theme and vision, despite the resistance of the sclerotic established order and its attachment to old habits and memories of the past. It is the force of this resistance that explains why competitors from another industry find it so easy to overtake the early front-runners—and why they

7 Arnold J. Toynbee, *A Study of History*, Oxford University Press, 1934.

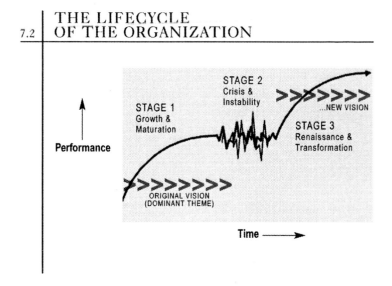

so easily displace old leaders. This is the genesis of the displacement phenomenon.

The displacement phenomenon

In this event, industry stagnation enables aggressive, quick-acting new rivals to depose the historic leaders. Often this occurs when leaders of established firms become complacent and fail to respond to a potentially disruptive technology.[8] These threats may be hard to see in the short term. But from the perspective of history, they often seem obvious! Let's consider some famous examples.

Ice-making

Ice harvesting was a thriving business in New England in the 1800s. Harvesters such as Frederic Tudor, America's first ice king, began cutting blocks of ice from Walden Pond in

---

8 Clayton M. Christensen cites examples from the disk drive, ink-jet printer, steel, and computer industries. See *The Innovator's Dilemma*, HarperBusiness, 1997.

Concord, Massachusetts, and shipping them, insulated in sawdust, around the world. In the nineteenth century, as iceboxes became common in U.S. homes, the search was on for cheaper and more reliable sources of ice. The new ice-making technology, based on the invention of the ammonia compressor in 1872, changed the industry. According to Ian Parker, the four artificial ice plants in 1860 increased in number to 200 by 1889 and to 2000 by 1909; ice now came from ice plants, not ponds and lakes.[9] But in the postwar period, home refrigerators and small ice machines drove most of the small block-ice companies out of business. As often happens when industry revolution occurs, neither ice harvesters nor icemakers, frozen in the puzzle of how to make sharper ice saws or freeze water faster, ever made it into the ranks of America's refrigerator manufacturers.[10]

Has the industry stabilized in modern times? Enter the Ice Factory. This computer-controlled system, introduced by the Packaged Ice company in 1992, lets grocery stores and convenience stores automatically make and package their own ice. An Ice Factory can produce, package, and store up to 40,000 bags of ice a year. This new technology has allowed Packaged Ice to become the leader in its industry, serving over 76,000 customers in 30 states. And by acquiring small competitors, Packaged Ice has been responsible for a rapid consolidation of the industry.

Ocean transport

A similar displacement phenomenon took place in the business of ocean transport, which flourished in the 19th century. The Yankee Clippers ruled the sea, and unlimited improvements in efficiency seemed possible. The Flying Cloud in 1852 set a new speed record: 374 nautical miles in 24 hours. In 1853, ship builders in New England launched 50 new clippers, but storm clouds were on the horizon. In 1807,

9 Ian Parker, "The Emperor of Ice," *The New Yorker*, February 12, 2001.

10 Guy Kawasaki, "Darwinism," *Forbes*, December 18, 1995.

Robert Fulton launched the first commercially successful steamboat, the 133-foot long Clermont, on the Hudson River. Then in 1854 the Panama Railroad opened, making a Cape Horn passage unnecessary.

But the leaders in the shipbuilding industry steadfastly attempted to improve speed without altering the basic design or introducing new technology. The typical sailing vessel went from a three-master with four sails in the 1850s to a four-master with five sails in the 1860s, and ultimately to seven masts with 55 sails in the 1890s, all for naught. Coal had replaced wind as the motive force for ocean transport, and no ship builder ever adapted successfully to the challenge of new competition. When coast-to-coast rail service began in 1869, the era of sail effectively had come to an end— shippers could now move goods by steam and rail from New York to San Francisco in only eleven days. A perceptive leader might have shifted to steam power, or even ultimately to the cruise-ship industry, where firms prosper by ferrying passengers around circular routes.

Buggy-Makers

The manufacturers of buggies in the 19th century were no more adept at learning from history. Among the hundreds of manufacturers of horse-drawn carriages, only a few had the foresight to see the potential impact of the automobile. In 1905 William C. Durant applied the assets amassed during his reign as head of the Durant-Dorn Carriage Company to acquire the Buick Motorcar Company.[11] Under Durant, Buick produced 750 cars in 1905, and 8,820 cars by 1908, second only to Ford. Durant used Buick as the nucleus for General Motors, which he formed in 1908 by merging Buick and Oldsmobile.[12]

---

11 The founder of the Buick Motor Car Company, David Dunbar Buick, was a failed entrepreneur. He owned a plumbing business that produced the first porcelain bathtub, and then moved into manufacturing engines for marine and stationary use. He founded Buick in 1903, but it was on the verge of demise when Durant bought the company.

Locomotives

For another example of displacement, look at the demise of Alco, the American Locomotive Company, which at one time was the market leader in the manufacture of steam-powered locomotives. It clung tenaciously to steam power as the motive force for its equipment, while General Electric and General Motors assumed leadership of the industry with their diesel engines, a technology that was available to all competitors as early as the end of the 19th century. Alco continued to ignore the greater efficiency of diesel technology. All that remains now of Alco's corporate headquarters in Schenectady, New York, is a Ramada Inn that displays photos of Alco locomotives.

Retailing

Montgomery Ward, the seemingly impregnable retailer, collapsed completely in 2001. Founded in 1872, this path-breaking enterprise operated strictly on mail orders placed from its famous catalog (they may have been America's first virtual store). Until 1926, Ward owned no retail stores. Analysts claim that Montgomery Ward never recovered from its reluctance to develop the retail market and its "depression-era principle of hoarding cash and avoiding expenditures wherever possible."[13] With its passing, Sears and discounters like Kmart became the leaders in consumer retailing. They,

---

12 Henry and Clement Studebaker opened a blacksmith and wagon shop in the 1850s to manufacture plows and other farm tools. They became a major producer of wagons and carriages, and eventually produced automobiles in a plant in South Bend, Indiana, until 1963.

13 The End of Montgomery Ward, *The New York Times*, March 2002.

in turn, have been displaced by Wal-Mart and Target, responding to consumers' increasing desire for value.[14]

In no industry can a business escape the threat of displacement by a new competitor. Leaders must offer products and services that meet customer needs—and customers are always on the hunt for better products and services at lower prices. Consider these other examples:

> Amazon.com, founded by Jeff Bezos in 1994, offered readers a virtual bookstore that challenged both book chains and small shops. Claiming an inventory of almost three million books, but selling only via the Internet, Amazon.com's customer-friendly website and overnight shipping enabled the disintermediation of the publishing industry.[15] Its current market share exceeds the sum of both Barnes & Noble and Borders, the leaders in retail book distribution.

> CNN, founded by Ted Turner in 1980, challenged the dominance of the network television giants (NBC, CBS, and ABC) in providing news to the public. By offering 24-hour service, it soon achieved a leading position in the coverage of world affairs, and inspired several imitators.

> Dell Computers, established in 1984 by Michael Dell, pioneered the selling of "mass-customized" computers directly to the consumer. In its 2001 fiscal year, revenues exceeded $80 billion as it continued to gain market share. Dell's inventory is now less than 7 days.

> FedEx, founded in Memphis in 1972 by Frederic Smith III, pioneered overnight delivery service, using its own fleet of airplanes and trucks. Their

---

14 Wal-Mart, Target, and Kmart all started in 1962; Kmart declared Chapter 11 bankruptcy in January 2002.

15 Disintermediation will occur in any industry when firms are able to serve the customer more efficiently without the participation of intermediate members of the value chain.

guaranteed next-day delivery attracted customers who were disenchanted by the slow and uncertain service provided by the U.S. Postal Service.

➤ GE and RCA seemed to have an unassailable position in consumer electronics in the 1950s and 1960s. GE assumed that replication of its widespread network of service centers would create an insuperable barrier to any new competitor. But the Japanese manufacturers such as Matsushita and Sony quickly outflanked GE by introducing appliances so reliable that they needed no service.

➤ Hewlett Packard's initiatives in low-cost personal printers eroded the apparent indispensability of the copying machine, a multibillion-dollar industry dominated by Xerox.

➤ Frieden and Underwood ruled the business-machine industry until the 1950s, but these leaders never even attempted to reinvent themselves. Thomas J. Watson built IBM into a major producer of time clocks and punched-card tabulators. But he then had the foresight to oversee its transformation into a goliath in the computer industry.

➤ Nucor recognized that steel production could be profitable if assets were reduced. By switching production to minimills that were relatively cheap to construct, the company became one of the largest U.S. producers, with sales in excess of $3 billion in 2001.

➤ Marriott, a company better-known as a hotel chain, is now positioned to compete with insurance companies that offer annuities by developing graduated care communities that assert "you can't outlive your assets."

The list of competitive displacements is endless. The lesson for all leaders is that they need to be prepared to either rapidly adapt or reinvent. As English philosopher Francis Bacon noted back in the 17th century, "He who will not apply new remedies must expect new evils, for time is the greatest innovator."

Yet adaptation is easier said than done, for leaders are often reluctant to adopt a new business model when the old model has served them so well. It is they, after all, who have the greatest investment and confidence in the old model and the least interest in change. Responsibility for initiating and managing change rests at the top of the organization, but kings and queens do not lead revolutions. Martin Van Buren illustrates the deep attachment that some leaders have to the status quo. In 1829, when he was still Governor of New York, he spoke eloquently to President Andrew Jackson on the threat to the Erie Canal barge business posed by the railroads. (Exhibit 7-3)

Leaders always have the option to go where no one has gone before—or not. Because most leaders of large hierarchical organizations view the prospect of change with consternation, they resort typically to strategies that improve efficiency and exploit existing competencies, rather than exploring new territory and inventing new business models. Well-known casualties of this syndrome include Wang Laboratories (forced to seek bankruptcy protection in 1992) and Digital Equipment Corporation (finally acquired by Compaq after failing to produce products for the personal computer market). Polaroid (too slow to introduce digital technology for photography) and Xerox (slow to revise its dependence on the copy machine model) are at high risk of failure. Another major potential victim of the displacement scenario is AT&T (itself the successor to Western Union and the dominant telecommunications player until the 1982 deregulation of the industry). Already under pressure from the regional telcos created in 1982, they face new pressure from wireless technology and its purveyors.

And add General Motors to the list. GM dominated the

7.3 | THE THREAT OF THE RAILROADS

Letter from Martin Van Buren, Governor of New York, to President Andrew Jackson, January 31, 1829

Dear President Jackson:

The canal system of this country is being threatened by the spread of a new form of transportation known as "railroads." The federal government must preserve the canals for the following reasons:

One. If canal boats are supplemented by railroads, serious unemployment will result. Captains, cooks, drivers, hostlers, repairmen, and lock tenders will be left without means of livelihood, not to mention the numerous farmers now employed in growing hay for horses.

Two. Boat builders would suffer, and towline, whip, and harness makers should be left destitute.

Three. Canal boats are absolutely essential to the defense of the United States. In the event of the unexpected trouble with England, the Erie Canal would be the only means by which we could ever move the supplies so vital to waging modern war.

For the above-mentioned reasons, the government should create an Interstate Commerce Commission to protect the American people from the evils of railroads and to preserve the canals for posterity. As you may know, Mr. President, railroad carriages are pulled at the enormous speed of fifteen miles per hour by engines, which, in addition to endangering life and limb of passengers, roar and snort their way through the countryside, setting fire to crops, scaring livestock, and frightening women and children. The Almighty certainly never intended that people should travel at such breakneck speeds.

---

auto industry for almost 70 years, but its market share has declined steadily from 48 percent in 1978 to 28 percent in 2000, with revenues of $185 billion. Ford, with revenues in 2000 of $170 billion, seems poised to take the top spot.[16] GM's recent decision to phase out the venerable Oldsmobile brand is one factor. But GM's malaise dates back to the 1970s, when it was slow to respond to the demand for small cars; the 1980s, when it overlooked the popularity of new aerodynamic

---

16 Although Ford's recent débacle with tires supplied by Firestone, its long-time partner, for Ford's Explorer SUV may delay its ascendancy to the top spot.

designs; and the 1990s, when it lagged in the SUV race. A culture that lacks accountability for failure hasn't helped.[17]

Managing the change process

Much of the stubborn reluctance to adapt to new business realities that we see demonstrated by leaders is the result of the cherished myth of stability: business as usual is a comforting notion, and organizations everywhere enjoy the illusion of safety that emerges when change is slow. As a result, it is common to find leaders directing themselves to preserving the status quo. In fact, corporations everywhere persist in trying to implement archaic strategies long after the world has changed.[18] Leaders rarely encourage debate about the alternatives—deliberately modifying the system or allowing it to evolve.

Implicit in this static world-view is another myth, the myth of control. Many leaders have the hubris to believe that they can control their environment, or at least those aspects of it that affect their organizations. Leaders of firms devoted to stability commit maximum effort to improving forecasts in the belief that they can erect defenses and marshal the resources required to cope with whatever comes. A corollary oversight is their failure to focus on alternative strategies. But their planners repeatedly forecast the wrong discontinuities and the future continues to remain perversely opaque. Stability is a false idol.[19] Firms that cling doggedly to old missions (the railroads) or old values (autocratic management) are especially vulnerable to extinction.

17 *The New York Times*, May 3, 2001.

18 In origami, the Japanese art of paper folding, the order and direction of the folds determine the form of the object that is created. An organization's destiny is similarly enfolded by its history and culture. See William Hall, *Management Science*, August 1984.

19 German philosopher and historian Oswald Spengler, in his 1923 classsic *Decline of the West* describes the world as consisting of "endless formations and transformations, the marvelous waxing and waning of organic forms."

20 Kurt Lewin, Martin Gold, *The Complete Social Scientist; A Kurt Lewin Review*, American Psychological Association, 1999.

A better policy for leaders is to abandon commitment to the status quo with all its deceptive stability, though changing course is hard to do when the firm is being successful. The total rigor and predictability of the endless status quo are exceedingly boring and enervating. Stable systems are fail-safe—they minimize the probability of failure by introducing high negative feedback to those who provoke change. Resilient systems, on the other hand, are safe-fail—they minimize the consequences of failure. And resilience and adaptability are much better survival skills

Leaders in a resilient system can often avoid the need for traumatic transformation by making periodic small creative adjustments. Riding a bicycle is a useful metaphor. We cannot predict which way the bicycle we are riding will fall if we lose our balance. But we can maintain its upright position by continuous adjustments of our body. In the organizational domain, adaptive leaders perform similar quick responses to the environment to maintain course and keep the system moving in the right direction.

Bill Gates, Microsoft's entrepreneurial Chairman, exemplifies this resilience and adaptability. The original Microsoft vision was "a computer in every home and on every desk" (all running Microsoft software). But Gates recognized the rapid surge of Internet technology as a threat to his software empire and quickly redirected resources to match the marketplace success of Netscape and others. And in 2001, finding that growth in personal computers was beginning to mature, Microsoft undertook a major initiative into a new consumer-market segment, positioning its Xbox hardware as a major play against Nintendo and its Gameboy console for the video game enthusiasts.

Jack Welch, GE's recently retired Chairman and CEO, provides us another impressive case history of transformation. He first tackled GE's high cost structure, massively downsizing its administrative overhead. Next came his mandate that every GE business needed to achieve industry leadership (#1 or a close #2) or face divestiture. "Boundarylessness" within the corporation became a keynote of the third reinvention, and in 1996 Welch introduced the six-sigma quality standard. The result to date has been continued growth, and GE has excelled among U.S. corporations in its contributions to shareholder value (although by other measures it has fared less well). Welch's successor, Jeffrey Immelt, inherits a daunting precedent. His specific challenges as GE's leader include recovering from Welch's ill-fated Honeywell merger, refurbishing an image tarnished by the PCB-pollution litigation, and slowing (or completing?) GE's evolution into financial-services, an industry change that would make the company potentially less attractive to investors.

Making adaptation happen

How do good leaders activate the process of adaptation or transformation? The challenge is to overcome the intrinsic resistance to change that every system demonstrates when at rest. In the terms described by sociologist Kurt Lewin, any system is frozen in a particular state.[20] To move it to a new state, leaders must first unfreeze the system, move it to a new position, and then apply appropriate forces to stabilize it.[21]

Physical and biological systems have much to teach us about the change process in organizations, and the alternatives to demise and extinction. What we denote as "reinvention" in a corporation has its analogy in nature's process of metamorphosis. A normal stage in the life history of many organisms, metamorphosis produces radical structural change in a short time. In social systems, like our corporations and

---

21 In thermodynamic terms, the system is inhibited from moving to a lower energy state by an activation energy barrier of magnitude Q.

other institutions, change more often comes about not by sudden transformation or revolution, which requires large amounts of energy, but by a slower process of nucleation and growth. A few leaders of change, such as the executive champions who are the nuclei of the new order, appear. If conditions are favorable, they attract partisans, their numbers multiply, and eventually they consume or transform (proselytize) the entire system. The probability that the transformation will succeed is a function of the number of change agents, their energy, and the resistance of the host (the strength of the antibodies). If the resistance to change is too great, the change agents will be discredited, rejected, or annihilated.

In a social system, like the corporation, adaptive leaders can often expedite change by using a meme, a term that denotes a unit of cultural information.[22] The meme is the equivalent in social systems of the gene in biological systems. Memes, however, may propagate horizontally (virally) as well as longitudinally, and they can breed diverse offspring. Memes can take the form of proverbs ("A stitch in time saves nine"), concepts, visions, technologies, and dominant themes. Even political systems (monarchy, communism, democracy) can be viewed as memes, and some systems have explicit memes, like Roosevelt's "New Deal" and Johnson's "Great Society." Ford's "Quality is Job #1" and Northwest Memorial Hospital's "Best Patient Experience" are corporate examples.

The leader's practical agenda for transforming an organization includes establishing a sense of urgency: using rhetoric to demonstrate that things will not get better—they will get worse unless we act (the sky is falling)—and that a little sacrifice will bring us to Shangri-La on the other side of the mountain. Once a sense of urgency has been conveyed, the leader must assemble a group of allies who will support the new vision and eliminate the obstacles to change. Professor Stan Abraham of California Polytechnic Institute

22 Richard Dawkin, *The Selfish Gene*, Oxford University Press, 1978.

reports on one effective nine-step change process: 1) create a vision, clear plan, and case for change, 2) identify actions that generate quick wins, 3) specify a new set of strategic values, 4) communicate the vision and change strategy, 5) overcome the resistance to change, 6) begin taking strategic actions, 7) begin sustaining the change, 8) inspire change throughout the organization, 9) create a culture of continuous change.[23] The logic for this sequence of events seems plausible. Unfortunately, the proof that simple algorithms for change really work needs more evidence.

Nevertheless, adaptive leaders recognize that change is inevitable. To avoid displacement by new competitors, they promote a culture that esteems and fosters change rather than opposing it, for they appreciate that the change process cannot be undertaken as a one-man or one-woman heroic effort. Adaptive leaders need to evangelize and proselytize—they need to establish a community that recognizes the importance of continual adaptation. It is this imperative that makes planning a leadership culture so important, a task to be addressed in the next chapter on the *guiding leader.*

---

23 Stan Abraham, "Conference Report," *Strategy and Leadership*, May, 2002.

Chapter 8

The Guiding Leader

Il faut cultiver notre jardin.
—Voltaire[1]

The leader's responsibility to ensure continuing high performance demands that he or she school a corps of respected individuals who share the values, purpose, vision, and strategy of the organization. Latent leaders, therefore, must be developed into actual leaders. Unfortunately, the science of replicating leaders is imperfect.

We don't know how many people have the potential to become leaders, but we do know that the world does not have an abundance of transformational leaders. Nevertheless, in every community there is an opportunity for such leaders to emerge—mayors, religious leaders, business leaders, media leaders, literary giants. Can we teach such men and women to be leaders? And to transform their organizations when conditions require it?

In the corporate world, we know that management can be taught—because the process of managing consists in applying a set of skills. We can teach anyone a skill, provided that he or she has a modicum of latent ability, the motivation to learn, and the willingness to practice. Operating from this premise, most corporations allocate significant funds to assess and develop managers. As further evidence for our belief that we can create competent managers (or at least administrators),

1 We must cultivate our garden. (from *Candide*)

U.S. business schools awarded over 102,000 MBA degrees in 1998 alone.

In an obvious extension of these initiatives, over 500 colleges and universities now also offer programs or courses in leadership, and some of these, like the University of Richmond and the University of Nebraska, boldly offer degrees in leadership. For another example, the London Business School, advertising in the *Economist*, exhorts potential students to "enroll as a manager, emerge as a leader."

An enormous industry now exists on the proposition that a week or a month or a year in an intensive program can raise consciousness, change behavior, and transform managers into leaders. The Center for Creative Leadership generates over $30 million in annual revenues from its array of courses on leadership. Both Outward Bound and the National Outdoor Leadership School (NOLS) have offered experiential programs for many years; graduates of the NOLS programs now exceed 40,000. For those in the workplace, the Internet currently shows almost two million matches for "leadership programs."

How are these programs supposed to work? Typically they begin by subjecting participants to a barrage of psychological tests intended to provide insights into leadership style and orientation. Unfortunately, the primary benefit of instruments such as the Myers-Briggs Type Indicator and FIRO-B is to provide participants with new vocabulary and taxonomy.[2] Managerial simulations and group projects conducted during most programs attempt to reinforce the merit of teamwork and better communications. Programs generally conclude after each participant has endured several sessions of mutual critique,

---

2 The FIRO-B (Fundamental Interpersonal Relations Orientation-Behavior) examines how individuals interact with one another, using inclusion, control, and affection as the principal variables. See Chapter 2 for a description of the Myers-Briggs instrument.

and everybody has prepared a set of resolutions ("I will give more positive feedback to my colleagues," "I will balance my work life and family life," etc.)

Despite the sparse data on the benefits of any of these programs, however, proponents of leadership training are evangelical in their fervor, citing enthusiastic testimonials from recent graduates as evidence of their effectiveness. But notwithstanding the tears of anguish or joy experienced by participants, these programs are no more effective than the T-groups and encounter session of the 1960s and 1970s.

Formal leadership programs may make us feel good (or challenged), but they do not reliably produce real change in our psyches or our conduct. They may heighten our awareness of the behavioral patterns of others, but they cannot replicate the environment and the time required to reshape our own behavior. As a result, fundamental behavior change is rare, and graduates often regress to old behavior patterns within weeks. These would-be leaders may have polished some skills, particularly in the area of communications, and they may have developed greater awareness of how they present themselves to others. But true leadership demands much more. Leadership is simply not a craft that schools can teach; leadership can only be developed in the crucible of organizational experience.

Why is this? If leadership simply entailed particular skills and knowledge, it might be easy to teach managers to become leaders. After all, anyone can learn the theory of leadership (i.e., *what* leadership is) by reading this book! But teaching men and women to *exhibit* the qualities and behavior of leaders (i.e., *how* to lead) is another matter. Leaders must create a structure and environment in which leaders-in-training can thrive—they must guide candidates along the path to leadership. To improve leadership continuity and succession demands a three-stage program: selection, challenge, and mentoring. Carrying out this program is the charge of the guiding leader.

Stage I—Selection

> For many are called, but few are chosen.
> —St. Matthew, *The Bible*

To develop new leadership, those who currently lead an organization must first select those individuals who have the potential to become leaders. This is not a task that can be delegated to the human-resource function of an organization. Only current leaders have the perspective to recognize novice leaders. Some men and women are destined to become followers, for they lack the motivation or interest to invest the time and energy to become leaders. But some people do surprise us with their leadership potential.

Akira Kurosawa, the great Japanese film-maker, focuses on the challenge of developing leadership in his brilliant production of *Kagemusha* (the shadow warrior). Set in 16th-century Japan, Kurosawa's story describes how Shingen, the dying leader of the Takeda clan, recruits a double to keep his imminent death secret from his enemies. The unlikely recruit is a convicted thief, about to be crucified for his crimes. After Shingen dies, his retainers decide to prolong the subterfuge. The double begins to show unexpected potential, however, and he becomes the true clan leader—he learns to embody Shingen's credo to "be like a mountain." The shadow warrior has reached into his own depths to discover and develop his leadership potential.

Singling out those men and women who are latent leaders to be groomed for leadership roles is an obligation of leaders that dates back to Plato. In the 5th century B.C., he advocated the training of men who would eventually lead the state in roles as philosopher-kings. According to Plato, potential rulers in a just society would first serve an apprenticeship in which they acquired the necessary skills, including a mastery of philosophy. Plato avers that "Unless philosophers become kings in our cities, or unless those who are kings and rulers become philosophers, I believe there can be no end of troubles in our cities."[3]

In my judgment, candidates for future leadership roles must meet three criteria:

Motivation. Potential leaders must exhibit a strong need to achieve (and a history of taking initiative) as well as a drive for power. Such men and women often have a "redemptive urge." Those who lack this fervor and the willingness to make an extended commitment to the leadership path are not likely to succeed.

Attitude. The evidence suggests that the inspirational force of leaders can be sustained only if the leader evinces optimism in the face of adversity. Resilience and adaptability are key virtues for apprentice leaders.

Morality. Devils and crooks lead us astray rather than down the path of long-term commercial success, often with devastating results. Potential leaders must have positive values and benevolent motives.

Stage II—Challenge

> Sweet are the uses of adversity.
> —Shakespeare, As You Like It.

Leadership is dormant until possible leaders have the opportunity to display their mettle in specific situations. An infusion of leadership theory is not enough—practice is essential. We cannot teach men and women to drive a car or shoot a game of pool (or a man to shave with a straight razor) with didactic instruction only; a hands-on trial-and-error process is necessary to learn. So in practice, leaders who want to develop successors must present them with challenges—learning experiences—for them to confront, struggle through, and grow from. And perhaps paradoxically, men and women have always acknowledged that failure in meeting such

---

3 Plato, *The Republic.*

challenges can provide important insight into more effective future leadership.

Challenges are sometimes thrust upon those who seek to become leaders—sudden changes in the market, the economy, the political or regulatory climate. An environmental or societal crisis—the Exxon Valdez oil spill in Alaska; the Union Carbide chemical-plant spill in Bhopal, India; the Tylenol cyanide-contamination incident; the fatal crashes caused by Ford/Bridgestone tires—often provides a crucible in which leadership can be tested. Without the prior experience of taking a risk and facing potential failure, crises can paralyze leaders rather than galvanize them.

This explains in part why many highly structured, risk-averse enterprises (like Allied Signal, IBM, and MetLife) recruit new transformational leadership from elsewhere. Boards of directors, observing evidence that the firm's business model is not working, often respond by seeking a proven leader to revitalize the enterprise. Struggling automaker Chrysler hired Lee Iacocca in 1978, for example. With the help of a government loan, he turned the company around, introduced the minivan and the K-car line, and repaid the loan in five years. Some other recent examples include Louis Gerstner at computer giant IBM and Gilbert Amelio at Apple Computer (since deposed and replaced by founder Steve Jobs)

Thus, the leader who wishes to nurture others in the art of leadership must place challenging tasks before them and must encourage potential leaders to step forward and practice leading, even when often the outcome may be failure. Contemporary French sociologist Pierre Bourdain suggests that everyone enters adult life with a "habitus," a predisposition to succeed or fail resulting from deeply engrained experience. Success, then, is not simply a function of skill, but is determined by practice, encouragement, and expectations of success. This same habitus will affect a leader's ultimate effectiveness.

A good model for the leadership training process comes

from the field of medicine. Surgical training, for example, is based on a classical sequence for procedures: see one, do one, teach one. In top surgical departments, leaders start with interns who have no experience in surgery, spend years training them, and then recruit faculty from the same ranks. And as in the case of many other professions, top performers distance themselves from average performers by practicing more assiduously. The moral for leaders who wish to develop a legacy is this: give apprentices as much practice as possible, in the process learn a great deal from teaching them.

Men and women may also step up voluntarily to take on a leadership challenge, like the legendary hero Theseus, who went into the labyrinth of the Minotaur. Or they may be forced by circumstances to face a major leadership challenge as in the case in modern times of President Harry Truman when he had to decide whether to deploy the atomic bomb against Japan in 1945.

Sometimes, of course, leadership is less deliberate. John F. Kennedy replied ironically to the question of how he became a hero: "It was involuntary. My boat was sunk." Of course he then rallied his crew, hauled a wounded man to safety, and then swam miles for help.

Stage III—Mentoring

> All rising to a great place is by a winding stair.
> —Francis Bacon

Teaching leadership is like teaching enlightenment—it is not possible by the direct conveyance of the Ten Commandments or the Eightfold Way, the Buddhist prescription for attaining Nirvana. However, just as great spiritual leaders communicate the path to enlightenment, leaders in organizations can point the way for their pupils. This is the task of a coach or mentor, a person who motivates, educates, and leads by example.

Many leaders whom I've interviewed report that a mentor, someone to whom they could turn for advice and counsel, played a strong role in their development as leaders. In some cases, the mentors provided explicit advice on how to speak and how to behave, or how to deal with the ambiguity of some leadership dilemmas. In other cases, the mentors simply acted as role models.

This is a key point. Good leadership in the end depends primarily on what leaders do, not on their qualities or style. Therefore, to develop potential leaders in our organizations, we must model leadership behavior ourselves, so that our subordinates can actually observe leadership in action. And as our organizations and our world become more complex and unpredictable, we must encourage all the managers in our enterprises to become more self-managing and to assume more personal authority. For, as the philosopher Immanuel Kant observed many years ago, self-management is the necessary prerequisite to managing others.[4] Only then, if leaders are to perpetuate the organizations they have created (or maintained), can they train others in the art of leadership.

Unfortunately, rarely do we find that corporations pass the leader's mantle gracefully from one regime to the next.[5] More common is the turmoil displayed by major firms such as IBM, Westinghouse, Sears, Digital Equipment, General Motors, Apple and others, companies that appear not to have mastered the leadership succession process. This suggests that even if leadership can be taught, even successful corporations don't do it well. There are some exceptions, however.

GE is perhaps the best-publicized exemplar of good

4 Immanuel Kant, "What is Enlightenment," 1784.

5 In a monumental act of shortsighted leadership, the Ford Motor Company has now discontinued its leadership training program. Jacques A. Nasser, Ford's CEO since 1999, had set the cultivation of leaders within the company as a priority. Nasser was recently ousted from his position, and the corporation has questioned the investment in training programs that might have distracted employees from their regular jobs.

leadership training. The major indicator of success is that other corporations frequently use GE as a source for leaders. In 2001, for example, 3M hired GE executive W. James McNerney Jr. as its next CEO, while Home Depot recruited GE executive Robert Nardelli to run the company. GE's screening system for its future leaders incorporates the four "E's": energy, energize, edge, and execute. These refer to the energy to cope with the frenetic pace of change; the ability to excite the organization and inspire it to action; the edge of having the self-confidence to make the tough calls; and executing by always delivering, never disappointing.

The World Bank has adopted an open-learning approach to training leaders. Their new Executive Development Program encourages managers to become "active learners" by reinventing and re-appropriating policies—learning by themselves rather than through the tutelage of experts. Johnson and Johnson's leadership development process is based on the premise that leaders are developed mainly on the job, and that employees are responsible for their own development. [6]

In the role of the guiding leader, helping others to follow in your path is the surest strategy for ensuring a memorable legacy of achievement. However, we need to remember the important difference between learning about leadership and practicing leadership. The three-fold approach of selection, challenge, and mentoring will maximize the odds of success. The ultimate test for any leader is to manage the delicate balance between control of one's subordinates to minimize the number and magnitude of mistakes they make and letting go of control so that subordinates can experience fully the consequences of their own decisions.

But guiding others to follow us requires not only that we set examples with our behavior, but that we also manifest the qualities that characterize effective leadership. Identifying these qualities is the subject of Chapter 9 and the *virtuous leader.*

6 Robert M. Fulmer and Marshall Goldsmith, *The Leadership Investment*, Amacom,

Chapter 9

The Virtuous Leader

There is no such thing as a perfect leader
Either in the past or present, in China or elsewhere.
If there is one, he is only pretending, like a pig inserting
Scallions into its nose in an effort to look more like an
elephant.

—Liu Shao-Ch'i

Leaders need to instill a sense of values and purpose, they need to develop inspiring visions and a strategy to realize these visions, and build the community necessary to implement the strategy. In this chapter we return to a discussion of the traits displayed by effective leaders. The *virtuous leader* recognizes that he or she must develop and strengthen those qualities that support them in the leadership role.

Leadership qualities or attributes fall into two categories:

Intrinsic or genetic qualities. These may be assets (like height or intelligence) or liabilities (like skin color or gender.) Such qualities are immutable—they cannot be altered or disguised.

Extrinsic qualities. These qualities, unlike those that are inherited, can be acquired and developed. When they contribute to a leader's effective functioning, we label them as leadership virtues.

Research has shown a modest positive correlation between leadership success and certain genetic characteristics, such as physical attractiveness.[1] A stronger negative correlation can be shown between success and some other genetic qualities. Gender can be a serious handicap; women and other minorities are often passed over for leadership roles.

When I challenge executives in my leadership programs to produce a list of great leaders, they typically nominate political heads of state, military generals, and athletic coaches. Assertive males who are doers rather that thinkers invariably dominate the roster. When women are included, the designees such as Margaret Thatcher (former British Prime Minister), Catherine the Great (18th century Empress of Russia), Elizabeth I (the first woman to occupy the British throne), and Joan of Arc have many of the characteristics of male leaders. But leadership need not entail male machismo, and such leaders often sacrifice the opportunity to introduce more feminine and humanistic elements such as sensitivity, loyalty, and compassion into the leadership process.

Nevertheless, since most of our contemporary organizations are dominated by males, a bias toward assertiveness and rationality should not surprise us. Folklore positions men as the creators of wealth, while positioning women more as the distributors of wealth. (Witness the roles of Elizabeth Dole and Bernadine Healy, the two recent heads of the American Red Cross.)

Many men embrace stereotypes of women that include traits of weakness, passivity, and instability. Images of sexuality or the obligations of motherhood also complicate the relationship between men and women as leaders and followers. As a result, women experience serious handicaps in organizations in which the majority of their followers are

---

1 Dean Keith Simonton's summary of the characteristics of "great" historical figures is one of the most comprehensive. See *Greatness*, The Guilford Press, 1994.
2 Deborah Sontag, "Who Brought Bernadine Healy Down," *The New York Times Magazine*, December 28, 2001.

male, who may hold women to a different (and higher) standard of performance from men.

The recent débacle involving Bernadine Healy, CEO of the Red Cross for the period 1999-2001, reinforces this point. After she indicted her organization as having a "corporate culture steeped in silos, turf battles, gossip, and very little teamwork, no system of reward of consequence for performance," the board forced her to resign.[2] Healy's later retort to the board is rich in irony: "Maybe you wanted more of a Mary Poppins and less of a Jack Welch."

What is the genesis of this condition? In *A Room of One's Own*, novelist Virginia Woolf describes the exclusion of women from avenues of power. She argues that the historic denial of access by women to halls of learning has in turn denied them access to wealth and power—and hence to positions of leadership. These exclusions then evolve into traditions that are difficult to change, especially in a patriarchal society. A more valid contemporary hypothesis is that biology has predisposed women to nurture rather than aggressively compete.[3] Or that the moral education of women promotes love and care as virtues, rather than assertiveness and independence. This implies that women can lead effectively where cooperation and nurturing are more important as key success factors than competition and aggression. An interesting possibility, then, is that female nurturers, like fictional Kate Janeway, captain of the Starship Enterprise, may herald the leaders of the future.

The bias against women in many firms may explain why most successful women executives lead organizations comprised primarily of other women or who serve women customers. Examples include Anita Roddick, founder of the multimillion-dollar socially-conscious Body Shop; Frances Hesselbein, former head of The Girl Scouts of America; Mary Kay Ash, founder and president of Mary Kay Cosmetics; Estée

---

3 Dorothy A. Kramer-Kawasaki, private communication.
4 *The New York Times*, February 23, 2002.

Lauder, head of the $4B Estée Lauder Companies; and Andrea Jung, CEO of Avon, the $5.7B beauty-products firm.

Successful alteration of this old paradigm may well require that men demonstrate a little more courage in accepting the leadership of women (or other minorities). But clearly it demands that women demonstrate their effectiveness in leading organizations staffed largely by men. Cécile Bonnefond, new CEO of champagne producer Veuve Clicquot, observes that in the champagne industry women can be effective because of their attention to detail, deep involvement with the product, and strong personal relationships with customers.[4] Ironically, when women do make it to the top of a cosmetics firm or lingerie company, they aren't credited with having as much talent as if they were running a business in other industries.[5]

In addition, women need to improve their self images. One need only look at a recent compilation of essays about heroines—each selected by another woman—to understand the problem.[6] Two of the 30 selections (Eleanor Roosevelt and Margaret Thatcher) were legitimate national or political leaders; five (Marian Anderson, Martha Graham, Anna Pavlova, Gertrude Stein and Virginia Woolf) made their mark on society as artists. The rest? A collection of pop icons such as Twiggy, Mae West, Madonna, and Jenny McCarthy; self-fulfilling prophets such as Oprah and Jane Fonda; or Princess brides such as Grace Kelly, Lady Diana, and Carolyn Bessette.)

Role models like this do not bode well for the future of women in leadership roles. Hillary Rodham Clinton, U.S. Senator from New York, and Madeleine Korbel Albright, former U.S. Secretary of State, offer us better models in the political domain. And on a global scale, we begin to see some evidence that women are accepted as national leaders,

---

5 Robert J. Allio, "Helping more women reach the top jobs," *Strategy and Leadership*, May 2002.
6 Holly Brubach, "Heroine Worship," *The New York Times Magazine*, November 24, 1996.

9.1 | WOMEN AS POLITICAL LEADERS

Leader	Country	Title	Date elected to office
Khaleda Zia	Bangladesh	Prime Minister	2001
Jennifer Smith	Bermuda	Premier	1998
Tarja Halonen	Finland	President	2000
Megawati Sukarnoputri	Indonesia	President	2001
Mary McAleese	Ireland	President	1997
Vaira Vike-Freiberga	Latvia	President	1999
Dame Silvia Cartwright	New Zealand	Governor – General	2001
Mireya Moscoso	Panama	President	1999
Gloria Macapagal-Arroyo	Philippines	President	2001
Sila Maria Calderon	Puerto Rico	Governor	2001
Pearlette Louisy	Saint Lucia	Governor – General	1997
Mame Madior Boye	Senegal	Prime Minister	2001
Chandrika Kumaratunga	Sri Lanka	President	1994
Adina Bastidas	Venezuela	Executive Vice President	2000

although only 15 of the world's 236 countries are currently led by women. (Exhibit 9-1)

In the major corporations of America, however, women are dramatically underrepresented. Although women comprise 46.5 percent of the U.S. labor force, they comprise only 12.5 percent of the Fortune 500 corporate officers. And only four women head Fortune 500 companies! (Exhibit 9-2) Several other high-profile women, including Linda Wachner at Warnaco, the diversified apparel manufacturer; Diana Brooks at Sotheby's, the renowned auction house; and Jill Barad at Mattel, the global toy company have recently been ousted from their positions. The three high-profile women CEOs of large technologically sophisticated firms (Carly Fiorina of Hewlett-Packard, Anne Mulcahy of Xerox, and Patricia Russo of Lucent Technologies) face major challenges.

9.2 | WOMEN AS CORPORATE LEADERS

Leader	Firm	2001 Revenue (Billions)	Fortune 500 Rank
Carly Fiorina Chairman & CEO	Hewlett-Packard	$49	19
Andrea Jung Chairman & CEO	Avon	$6	310
Anne Mulcahy President & CEO	Xerox	$19	109
Patricia Russo President & CEO	Lucent Technologies	$41	28

There are, however, 9.1 million women-owned firms in the U.S., and those with greater than 100 employees are growing in number at six times the national average, suggesting that the pipeline is beginning to fill. OprahWinfrey and Martha Stewart are creating exciting media empires, and Meg Whitman has received major accolades for her performance as CEO of eBay, the on-line auction site.

Nevertheless, leaders do come in all sizes and shapes, notwithstanding evidence that tall, attractive, intelligent individuals are more likely to become leaders than those who are short, ugly, and stupid. John F. Kennedy was a charismatic and articulate U.S. President, while Pope John XXIII was "short, balding, stout, and significantly older."[7] In the five-year period after his election in 1958 at the age of 76, Pope John accomplished a dramatic restructuring and renewal of the Catholic Church, a venerable institution that had vigorously resisted any modification of dogma or ritual for centuries.

By and large then, the important traits and qualities that we see in the leaders of the world are not inherited—they

7 Walter Zultowski, *LIMRA's Vision*, April/May, 1996.

are developed. And these developed qualities are much more important than the genetic qualities. Inherited traits, for the most part, simply represent legacies to be overcome or leveraged. As a result, it's clear to me that leaders, assuming they possess a modicum of intelligence and talent, are made or developed. More accurately, *leaders make themselves*—they develop the qualities that enable them to be effective. They develop these essential qualities by performing leadership acts that demand the application of these qualities—by reinforcing a pattern of leadership behavior. They develop their latent leadership qualities, in other words, by practice, just as athletes and musicians do. Superior athletes need strength, endurance, coordination, and agility to excel. Accomplished musicians practice to develop their sense of rhythm and ear for melody.

The possession of a particular set of qualities will not inevitably produce a leader. As we have discussed previously, leaders need to govern in a particular style, and they need to acquire certain skills. But certain qualities are the prerequisite (necessary but not sufficient) to effective leadership.

Developing lists of important virtues has occupied philosophers as early as the Greek era. Aristotle proposed prudence, justice, courage and temperance as the four cardinal virtues. The Christians added faith, hope, and charity to the list. Some qualities—like wisdom, dignity, and will—are assets not only for leaders but for all men and women. Compiling a comparable catalog for leaders is a challenge, for as we examine the personality and behavior of leaders, we see enormous diversity. Every leader appears to have selected from a spectrum of qualities, reflecting the possibility of solving the leadership equation in many ways. Yet upon analysis, we find that every good leader acquired a cluster of specific traits or virtues to support them in the leadership role, although their relative importance may depend on the circumstances.

What are these differentiating virtues? In his or her role

9.3 THE LEADER'S ROLES AND QUALITIES

Leader's Role	Cardinal Leadership Quality
Establish values and purpose (what matters to us)	Character
Develop vision and direction (where must we go)	Creativity
Build community (how can we travel together)	Compassion

as a Purposeful Leader, concerned with values, purpose, and meaning, the individual acts with **character**: ethics, morality, integrity, are the foundation for decisions. In the role as Visionary or Strategic Leader, **creativity** is the key. Leaders conceive and initiate the changes that precede the attainment of new visions. Creativity forms the keystone for the leader's obligation to articulate a compelling vision for the organization. In acting as a Beneficent Leader, men and women act with **compassion** as they transform a group of individuals into a true community. Character, creativity, and compassion are the three cardinal leadership virtues. Exhibit 9-3 illustrates the relationship between these qualities and the leadership roles.

Character

> Every man's character is the arbiter of his fate
> —Publilius Syrus

Character is the first of the three cardinal qualities of a virtuous leader. The character traits of such leaders include integrity, morality, and authenticity. Integrity and morality form a platform that establishes justice and goodness as guiding principles for organizational decisions. These values enable the leader to answer with greater conviction the questions "What's important?" and "Why are we here?" An important additional component of the leader's character is authenticity, which gives credibility to the leader's behavior. And credibility gives power to the leader.

Abraham Lincoln shows us the importance of character in a leader. He faced a critical dilemma during his term of office—how could he outlaw slavery in the face of the right to property specified in the Constitution? Ultimately he resolved the question by concluding that slavery was morally wrong because it denied slaves their fundamental human rights.[8]

Prior to serving as President, Lincoln underwent a serious midlife crisis in 1849, when at the age of 40 he retired from public life, considering himself to be a failure as a lawyer and a politician. He resumed his career in 1854 after almost five years of isolation in which he sought his identity and prepared to create his ultimate legacy. When he returned, he exhibited "psychic radiance," stemming from what Tolstoy considered to be his "moral power and greatness of character."[9]

Not withstanding their political achievements, dictators such as Adolph Hitler, Joseph Stalin, and Slobodan Milosevic fail the test of character. They ignored the fundamentals of ethical behavior by treating people as means to an end. The ends, that is, the consequences of one's actions, are important, but they cannot be separated from the means. Mahatma Gandhi is an obvious exemplar of this principle.

In his discussion of why amoral leadership does not work, author James O'Toole cites Jack Welch's reign as an example of leadership that lacked integrity.[10] His evidence includes a litany of ethical misbehavior in GE: defense contracting overcharges, rigged test crashes of General Motors pickup trucks by NBC (a GE subsidiary), and accounting exaggeration of sales at GE's Kidder Peabody subsidiary. Yet GE's senior management claims

8 Abraham Lincoln, 1854 speech.
9 *The New York World*, February 7, 1909.
10 James O'Toole, *Leading Change*, Jossey-Bass, 1995.

integrity to be the "first and most important of our values. Integrity means always abiding by the law, both the letter and the spirit. But it's not just about laws; it is at the core of every relationship we have."[11] It's not hard to make the case that Welch and his colleagues are adherents to Machiavelli's policy: "A prince who desires to maintain his position must learn to be not always good, but to be so or not as needs require." During Welch's regime, pragmatism has clearly been more important than moral character, and GE's transgressions appear to reflect the inevitable consequences of an obsessive focus on shareholder value.[12]

Some other examples of character deficiency include Frank Lorenzo and William Agee. Lorenzo was a morally corrupt man who methodically destroyed Eastern Airlines. Agee was a victim of the pathology that can accompany power and the sycophantism that it promotes. In his role as Chairman of Morris Knudsen Corporation, an Idaho-based conglomerate, Agee was accused of flagrant mismanagement and personal excess. His directors finally ousted him in 1995. More recent candidates for flawed character include Kenneth Lay, recently-resigned Chairman of Enron, a mammoth energy trading company that captivated investors, and Jeff Skilling, his former CEO. Arrogance, greed, deceit, and financial chicanery permeated their leadership, and as a result Enron plunged into bankruptcy.[13] John Rigas of Adelphia and Dennis Koslowski of Tyco destroyed investor confidence by their acts of personal greed.

Some of our contemporary leaders appear to contradict the thesis that character matters. But great leaders define their own values, and in some cases they exhibit behavior that society deems immoral. In their private lives, Franklin Delano Roosevelt, John F. Kennedy, Martin Luther King, Jr., Bill Clinton and Jesse Jackson have all been criticized for

---

11 General Electric, Annual Report, 2000.
12 An excessive span of control also contributes to communications gaps and loss of control.
13 Bethany McLean, "Why Enron Went Bust," *Fortune*, December 24, 2001.

their sexual improprieties. Their lack of fidelity undoubtedly compromised some of their effectiveness, although Bill Clinton's popularity with his constituents remained high even after his impeachment for perjury in December 1998.

Character and morality alone, unfortunately, do not produce outstanding leadership, as witness U.S. President Jimmy Carter—a profoundly moral man who lacked other critical leadership qualities and skills. During his term in office, Carter proposed no new social programs, and a hostile Congress ignored many of his initiatives, such as tax reform and reduction of the government bureaucracy. He left office frustrated and disappointed, although his subsequent behavior as a leader in the quest for peace has been impressive.

Nevertheless, although private virtue alone does not assure public prowess, outstanding leaders always distinguish themselves by their character.

Creativity

> Those who dance are thought mad by those who do
> not hear the music.
> —Hopi saying

Creativity is the second of the cardinal leadership virtues. It informs all of a leader's actions, but it is particularly relevant to individuals in their roles as Visionary and Strategic Leaders.[14]

As they answer the questions "Where do we need to go?" and "How will we get there?", leaders see possibilities that their predecessors have ignored or rejected. Leaders have bold visions, and creativity enables this boldness to emerge. Awareness (mindfulness) and openness (the ability to look at old situations with new eyes) are corollary traits that enable creativity to manifest.[15]

---

14 Leaders are more like poets than plumbers; leadership is an aesthetic process that requires great creativity.

As Jean Paul Sartre notes, "Before Renoir painted, there were no Renoir women in Paris; now you see them everywhere." A fresh perspective is invaluable, and leaders show us a different reality—they transform our world with their visions.

In reviewing the characteristics of the American President, historian Henry Adams notes that he "resembles the commander of a ship at sea. He must have a helm to grasp, a course to steer, a port to seek." [16] Great Presidents possess (or are possessed by) a vision of an ideal America. They have dreams—for instance, FDR and the New Deal; LBJ and the Great Society. Lincoln replaced his early vision of preserving the Union with a far more compelling vision: freedom for all. All great leaders have a passion to make sure that the ship of state sails on a right course, one that connects with the needs, anxieties, and dreams of the people.

Creativity is nurtured by curiosity, the willingness to seek out new technology and new methods. Only novices feel bound by the old rules. Dick Fosbury's new technique for the high jump, subsequently known as the "Fosbury Flop" required a backward jump after the approach to the bar. When he broke the high-jumping record at the 1968 Olympics in Mexico City with a leap of 7 feet 4 inches, he changed every athlete's approach to the bar. Fosbury made up his own rules, one of the hallmarks of a leader.

Visions lie dormant, of course, unless the leader has courage and is willing to take risk. Most entrepreneurs display this quality. But in many mature firms, risk aversion is the dominant ethos. This explains in part the data in Chapter 7 that show innovation most often taking place outside these firms or their industry.

15 "In the beginner's mind there are many possibilities, but in the expert's mind there are few." Shunryu Suzuki, *Zen Mind, Beginner's Mind*, John Weatherhill, Inc., 1979.

16 Arthur M. Schlesinger, Jr., "The Ultimate Approval Rating," *The New York Times Magazine*, December 15, 1996.

17 The episode later became the subject of Alfred Lord Tennyson's epic poem.

The willingness to risk is different from foolhardiness. During the siege of Sevastopol in October 1854, Lord Cardigan led his British Light Brigade of cavalry directly into the face of the Russian field batteries. We admire the élan of the charge—but the Russians decimated the British brigade.[17] In a similar incident, the Confederate troops of Major-General George Pickett mounted a futile charge on Cemetery Ridge, where they suffered devastating losses from Federal artillery and musket fire. Leaders must avoid a rash course of action that commits them to failure, when an alternative strategy would be better.

Risk is part of any creative process, for we never can predict the final outcome, and leadership is no exception. The elders in Native American tribes give this advice to young men as they prepare for their initiation into manhood: "At some point in your life you will come to a great chasm. Jump. It is not as wide as you think."[18] Great leaders jump over what others perceive to be great chasms.

The precursor to taking risks is a positive attitude. Leaders believe that they will succeed.[19] Psychologist Martin Seligman differentiates between optimists and pessimists. Optimists believe that bad events are temporary, are limited to a specific situation, and are not our fault—they are caused by bad luck, circumstances, or other people. Pessimists, on the other hand, believe that bad events endure and undermine life—and that these bad events are our own fault. Optimists do better in school, work, and sports; they get promoted and elected to office; and they are healthier. Pessimistic people give up early and become depressed.[20]

18 Hal Zina Bennett, *Zuni Fetishes*, Harper, 1993.
19 Warren Bennis describes the Wallenda Factor, named after Karl Wallenda, the famous high-wire artist who never fell until the day in 1978 when he began to worry about falling before he attempted to traverse a 75-foot tight rope in San Juan, Puerto Rico. See *An Invented Life*, Addison Wesley, 1993.
20 Martin E.P. Seligman, *Learned Optimism*, Pocket Books, 1998.

The source of pessimism is learned helplessness in the face of adversity (see the parable of *The Man and His Stone*— Exhibit 9-4). Fortunately, pessimism is not irreversible. Just as we learn to be pessimistic, we can learn to be optimistic. Our lives begin in total helplessness, but gradually we can learn to take control. Leaders have learned to be optimists.

9.4 | **A MAN AND HIS STONE**

One stormy night, a man came upon a monastery in the forest. He knocked at the thick door and shouted to be admitted for quite some time, but no one responded. Finally, he found a heavy stone and pounded upon the door. A monk appeared and directed him to a room containing only a sleeping mat. Exhausted, and relieved to be out of the rain, the traveler put his stone on the floor and fell asleep.

In the morning when he awakened, he tried to open the door of his room to ask for food, but the door was locked. He shouted, but no one answered. At last, he picked up his stone and pounded on the door. A monk soon appeared and led him into another room, where food, water, and a pallet were waiting. The traveler bathed, ate, and rested.

Once again he sought to leave. Once again he found the door locked, and no one answered his call. When he pounded with the stone, he was again answered and taken to a more comfortable room.

And so he went for a number of days, carrying his heavy stone from room to room, and using it to open each succeeding door. Ultimately, he no longer shouted or tried to open the door, but immediately pounded with his stone when he wanted to leave.

One day, when he was pounding heavily on a door, the monk on the other side said to him, "Why don't you try the door yourself?" The man pushed against the door, and it opened easily into the next room.

The monk asked, "Must you always carry your heavy stone and beat upon the doors? There are many that are not locked."

Adapted from the Zen literature by the author.

Compassion

Some apparent leadership virtues, like tenacity, can be used in the service of immoral causes. But not compassion, the third of the cardinal virtues for the leader.[21] Leaders with compassion

---

21 Compassion was the principal virtue of Confucianist China, where it was

view members of the community as significant elements in the success of the enterprise. This compassion serves as the antidote to the leader's temptation to coerce using the power of his or her position. It is the virtue that supports the leader in the role as a builder of the community, as he or she addresses the question of how we can collectively achieve our visions and realize our aspirations. Closely related qualities include empathy, charity, magnanimity, and providentiality—a deep concern for the welfare of the community as a whole.[22]

Compassion is a more potent virtue than emotional intelligence, the current catch-all term used to describe the social and interpersonal competencies that underlie compassion.[23] The emotional intelligence model comprises four core domains: self-awareness, self-management, social awareness, and relationship management. A set of eighteen skills purport to support each of these domains. In the domain of social awareness, for example, the three important competencies are empathy, organizational awareness, and service to the client or customer. The emotional intelligence model bears strong resemblance to the ideas of Dale Carnegie (*How to Win Friends and Influence People*) and suffers badly from the absence of any empirical correlation with leadership effectiveness. A simpler model was proposed in 1985 by Robert Sternberg, who suggested that intelligence consisted of three parts: analytic intelligence, creative intelligence, and practical intelligence (skill in everyday living and adapting to life's demands.)[24]

---

expressed as *Jen*. *Jen* is considered to be the supreme virtue of Confucian ethics, representing the epitome of human qualities. It includes *chung* (faithfulness to oneself and others) and *shu* (altruism).

22 J. Sterling Livingston suggests that both empathy and a need for power are prerequisites for leadership. See "The Myth of the Well-Educated Manager," *Harvard Business Review*, Jan-Feb 1971.

Compassionate behavior depends critically on effective communication. It is especially important that the leader listen empathetically to the voices of the community. (Listening to the voices of change is a wonderful leadership aptitude.) The Buddhist term for this particular skill is "bare attention." When I listen to you with bare attention, you realize that I am fully attentive, not only to the words you speak, but to the full emotional and psychic content of your message. Listening to you while I simultaneously formulate a response falls short of this standard.

Failure to communicate can have tragic outcomes. At Babcock & Wilcox, a major manufacture of industrial equipment, Paul Craven, head of the firm's power generation division, was unable to meet a major customer's schedule for the delivery of reactor pressure vessels. Although Craven was devoted to the company, he felt that he lacked the authority, budget, and staff to perform. Yet he clung obstinately to the belief that he could individually solve the division's problems. In 1968, the day before a scheduled review with George Zipf, the company president, Craven climbed into a dry bathtub in Akron's luxurious Carlton House, where his chauffeur found him the next morning. Craven had slashed his ankles, cut his own throat, and stabbed himself in the heart with the 8-inch blade of a butcher knife.

In yogic psychology, the trait of compassion is found at the fourth chakra, the subtle energy center of the heart. Leaders who are attached to the third chakra, the center of ambition and the will to power, are unrealized as leaders. Dictators such as Napoleon, Stalin, and Hitler are deluded by dreams of glory that emanate from a fixation on power. Those who have evolved to the higher fourth chakra will exhibit compassionate unity with their followers, as illustrated by the *Heaven and Hell* parable.

23 Daniel Goleman, Richard Boyatzis, and Annie McKee, *Primal Leadership; Realizing the Power of Emotional Intelligence*, Harvard Business School Press, 2002.

Heaven and Hell [25]

The rabbi had a conversation with the Lord about Heaven and Hell. " I will show you Hell," said the Lord, and led the rabbi into a room containing a large group of famished, desperate people sitting around a large circular table. In the center of the table rested an enormous pot of stew, more than enough for everyone. The smell of the stew was delicious and made the rabbi's mouth water. Yet no one ate. Each diner at the table held a long-handled spoon, long enough to reach the pot and scoop up a spoonful of stew, but too long to get the food into one's mouth. The rabbi saw that their suffering was indeed terrible and bowed down his head in compassion.

"Now I will show you Heaven," said the Lord, and they entered another room, identical to the first—same large, round table, same enormous pot of stew, same long-handled spoons. Yet there was gaiety in the air: everyone appeared well-nourished, plump, and exuberant. The rabbi could not understand and looked to the Lord. "It is simple," said the Lord, but it requires a certain skill. You see, the people in this room have learned to feed each other!"

Leadership deficiencies

No leader is perfect—the ideal leader is an abstraction, a Platonic form that we can only imagine. (Kant cautions that "out of the crooked timber of humanity, no straight thing can ever be made.") All leaders are in the process of developing the qualities needed to improve their effectiveness as leaders, which is to say that all leaders exhibit defects of personality. Minor flaws may not interfere with the successful discharge

24 Robert Sternberg, *Handbook of Intelligence*, Cambridge University Press, 2000.

of the leader's role. We can learn a great deal about leadership, however, by examining what causes leaders to lose their way. The primary source of errant leadership behavior is pride and arrogance, which encourages leaders to lose touch with reality and changing times. Not a few leaders exhibit a pathology of narcissism. According to the American Psychiatric Association, such leaders display a pervasive pattern of grandiosity, a need for admiration, and a lack of empathy.[26] Sinful pride causes many saints to become Lucifers. Historian Barbara Tuchman provides some cogent examples of the resulting leadership folly:

Why did the Trojan rulers drag that suspicious-looking wooden horse inside their walls despite every reason to suspect a Greek trick? Why did successive ministries of George III insist on coercing rather than conciliating the American Colonies, though repeatedly advised by many counselors that the harm done must be greater than any possible gain? Why did Charles XII and Napoleon and successively Hitler invade Russia despite the disasters incurred by each predecessor? Why did Montezuma, master of fierce and eager armies and of a city of 300,000 succumb passively to a party of several hundred alien invaders, even after they had shown themselves all too obviously human beings, not gods? Why does American business insist on "growth" when it is demonstrably using up the three basics of life on our planet—land, water, and unpolluted air?[27]

These leaders, and many like them, suffered from *akrasia*—knowing what is best but refusing to do it. Overcome by pleasure, fear, love, hate, or passion, they lead their trusting followers down the road to perdition.

As the Greek myths have also shown us, hubris leads to tragedy. Icarus, escaping from Crete on artificial wings constructed from feathers by his father Daedalus, ignored

25 A Hasidic parable cited by Irwin Yalom, *The Theory and Practice of Group Psychotherapy*, Basic Books, 1995.

26 *Diagnostic Statistical Manual of Mental Disorders IV*, American Psychiatric Association, 1994.

the warnings not to fly too close to the sun. When the wax on his wings melted, he plummeted into the Aegean Sea.

A similar tragedy is the case of Ken Olsen, Founder of the Digital Equipment Company, the leading producer of minicomputers in the 1970s and 1980s, Olsen refused steadfastly to accept the growing customer interest in personal computers. He clung obstinately to the company's proprietary VAX operating system, until the opportunity to play in the personal computer market had passed. As a result, Digital passed into stagnation and ultimate decline. The board ousted him in 1992, and Compaq acquired the remains of the company in 1998.

Virtuous leaders develop and nurture the cardinal qualities of character, creativity, and compassion through practice. As they become more comfortable with each attribute, they find it easier to exhibit the behavior necessary to provide purpose and meaning to the enterprise, establish a compelling vision and sense of direction, and build a strong community. The leader may suggest other virtues, such as courage, moderation, and wisdom. I do not dispute that these may be complementary virtues. But starting with character, creativity, and compassion gives any individual a powerful head start in the quest for leadership.

How can we evaluate the performance of leaders? The best metric is the legacy of their ideas and the organizations they lead. This will be our next subject.

27 Barbara W. Tuchman, *The March of Folly, From Troy to Vietnam*, Ballantine Books, 1984.

Chapter 10

Evaluating Leaders and Leadership

To recognize a leader is not always easy, for leaders do not necessarily reveal themselves by the force of their personality or the acclaim of a multitude of followers. Furthermore, today's leaders no longer exhibit the heroic (and usually autocratic) characteristics of leaders from an earlier era. The reason is straightforward: heroic leadership no longer works, and respectable business journals like *The Economist* are gloating over the "overthrow of celebrity CEOs."[1] Except in totalitarian systems, men and women demand a voice in the decisions that may affect their future welfare.

Our theory of leadership distinguishes two categories of leaders: those whose impact is indirect and often unintentional—the artists, writers, and intellectuals who typically influence their followers from a distance (like physicist Albert Einstein, economist John Maynard Keynes and management writer Peter Drucker) and those who interact directly with their followers in an enterprise or institution, be it political, athletic, military, or corporate.

Given the benefit of a historical perspective, it's easy to formulate lists of leaders— men and women who have had a significant and memorable impact on their followers and their times. Every classic or contemporary author writing on the subject of leadership boldly proposes a list of leadership exemplars (Exhibit 10-1).

---

1 *The Economist*, May 4, 2002.

| 10.1 | HISTORICAL NOMINEES FOR LEADERSHIP |

Carlyle's Heroes[1]

Odin	(Divinity)
Mahomet	(Prophet)
Dante, Shakespeare	(Poet)
Luther, Knox	(Priest)
Johnson, Rousseau, Burns	(Man of Letters)
Cromwell, Napoleon	(King)

Burns' Revolutionary Leaders [2]

Mao Tse Tung
Woodrow Wilson
Simon Bolivar
Ho Chi Minh
Vladimir Lenin
Mahatma Gandhi

Gardner's Eleven Leaders[3]

Margaret Mead
J. Robert Oppenheimer
Robert Maynard Hutchins
Albert P. Sloan, Jr.
George C. Marshall
Pope John XXIII
Eleanor Roosevelt
Martin Luther King Jr.
Margaret Thatcher
Jean Monnet
Mahatma Gandhi

O'Toole's Rushmoreans[4]

George Washington
Thomas Jefferson
Abraham Lincoln
Franklin Roosevelt

[1] Thomas Carlyle, *On Heroes, Hero-worship, and the Heroic in History*, University of California Press, 1993.
[2] James MacGregor Burns, *Leadership*, Harper & Row, 1978.
[3] Howard Gardner, *Leading Minds*, Basic Books, 1995.
[4] James O'Toole, *Leading Change*, Jossey-Bass Publishers, 1995.

In the absence of historical perspective, identifying contemporary leaders is a more daunting undertaking. Some possible candidates from the political domain might include Daw Aung San Suu Kyi, the 1991 Nobel peace prize recipient from Burma (Myanmar), who led the movement for human rights and the restoration of democracy in her country. She has unfortunately been under virtual house arrest since 1996. Pressure from an international financial aid boycott recently accomplished her release. Deng Xiaoping began his program of modernization and economic reform in China in 1978, reforms badly needed after the excesses of the Cultural Revolution. His tenure was marred by the repression of pro-democracy movements, the most notorious in June 1989 at Tiananmen Square. Kofi Annan, the Ghana-born United Nations Secretary-General, was recently elected to an unopposed second term. He improved decision-making and amity within the U.N. Nelson Mandela and Desmond Tutu, South Africans who successfully fought the inequities of apartheid, surely qualify as leaders.

Often, as in the case of a leader who helps an organization transcend a crisis (Winston Churchill in England during World War II, or former Mayor Rudy Giuliani in New York City after the September 2001 terrorist attack on the World Trade Center), they are highly visible. But some good leaders may be hard to recognize, for their leadership is imbedded in the fabric of the organization. This is why a better model for leadership than GE may be an organization like 3M. This diversified corporation has grown consistently since its founding in 1892. But as contrasted with the ruthless pruning of people, products, and businesses carried out by Jack Welch at GE to achieve his vision, we find a series of low-profile chairmen (Lew Lehr, Allen Jacobson, L.D. DeSimone) who nurtured a culture that capitalized on micro-innovation.

The metrics for leadership

How can we evaluate the contribution of leaders and distinguish between the great, the good, and the mediocre? How will your colleagues, stockholders, employees, and other stakeholders assess your effectiveness as a leader? How will history judge you? Let's consider the possibilities:

Task completion

Getting the job done (implementing strategy) is the purview of the manager, not the leader. Those who accomplish a specific task are at best ordinary leaders, those who engage in a series of transactions with followers—for example, this wage for that service. John F. Kennedy observed cynically that some of his greatest predecessors received credit for doing things when they could have done nothing else. But doing only what others expect is a far cry from leading with inspiration!

Longevity

Longevity is rare among leaders; reigning for years in a changing world demands exceptional skill. Unfortunately, long terms of office, when they do occur, are often associated with organizational atrophy and inertia. We admire Queen Victoria more for the duration of her 63-year reign (from 1837 to 1901) than for any major contributions she made to the British Empire. And Elizabeth I has just celebrated her 50th year as Queen! Fidel Castro has misruled Cuba for over 40 years (since 1959), transforming it into a socialist state that has suffered continuing economic decline. Corporate examples of the perils of long tenure include Ken Olsen at Digital Equipment.

In some cases, to be sure, longevity can be beneficial, for it gives a leader ample time to establish a culture that perpetuates strategic momentum. Lee Kuan Yew, Singapore's Prime Minister from 1959 to 1990, led his country through a transition from a Malaysian adjunct to a powerful Asian economic city-state. And in the corporate domain, Warren Buffet of Berkshire Hathaway, Herb Kelleher at Southwest

Airlines, and Sam Walton at Wal-Mart illustrate the occasional benefits of longevity. In general, however, we cannot correlate the effectiveness of a leader with his or her longevity.

Popularity

I find little relationship between the popularity of leaders and their effectiveness. Warren Harding, the 29th U.S. President, was immensely popular, yet today he is unanimously deemed to be a failure; he lacked vision, and people today remember his administration primarily for its corruption. Ronald Reagan achieved similar popularity, but few will remember his achievements.

Harry S. Truman, in comparison, garnered only a 31% approval rating at the end of his tenure as the 33rd U.S. President from 1945 to 1953. Yet many historians today place him in the near-great category. He centralized decision-making ("The buck stops here!") and became the architect of the Fair Deal social programs. Among his other initiatives were the Marshall Plan (1948) and the Truman Doctrine (1947), which was aimed at containing communism. His controversial decision to drop the atom bomb on Japan in August 1945 brought an end to the war. Truman may well have been the prototype of the non-charismatic leader.

Great leaders do not necessarily obey the wishes of their followers—they act in ways that are consistent with their own vision, even if the followers do not yet comprehend or embrace it. Plato tells the story of the leader who leaves his followers behind in the cave as he or she seeks enlightenment. (see Appendix 10-A) Those in the cave are content to view false images of reality, displayed on the cave wall as shadows (just as their modern counterparts have become entranced by Excel spreadsheets). When the leader returns, they shun him or her.

In our times, forceful leaders who assume a strong position on hotly-debated issues often distance themselves from their followers and those who profit from maintaining the status quo.[2] Many such leaders lose popularity almost overnight, as when the British abandoned Winston Churchill after World War II. Iron Lady Margaret Thatcher, the first woman to serve as Prime Minister of the United Kingdom (1979-90), was a strong advocate of privatization and withdrawal of the government from intervention in the economy. But dissatisfaction with her taxation policies forced her to step down. Indira Gandhi, Prime Minister of India from 1966-77 and 1980-84, was no more popular, particularly during the emergency years. Many viewed her as a dictator who sacrificed democracy for personal power, and she was assassinated by her Sikh guards in 1984.

Such leaders must be imbued with a sense of personal expendability; they must be prepared to sacrifice themselves if the best interests of society require it.[3] In the extreme, a leader, like Joan of Arc, the Maid of Orleans, may accept martyrdom on behalf of his or her cause. Inspired by religious visions, she organized the French resistance against the English in 1429. But the Burgundians sold her to the English, who tried her for heresy and burned her at the stake. A more contemporary example may be Palestinian Yasir Arafat, perhaps an aspiring martyr.

Good leaders, then, may or may not be popular. Some popular leaders were fools, while some spurned leaders changed the course of history.

---

2 "Is it so bad, then, to be misunderstood? Pythagoras was misunderstood, and Socrates, and Jesus, and Luther, and Copernicus, and Galileo, and Newton, and every pure and wise spirit that ever took flesh. To be great is to be misunderstood." Ralph Waldo Emerson, *Self Reliance*, 1841.

3 Socrates is our archetypal case of expendability. The Athenians indicted him on vague charges of impiety and corrupting the youth and subsequently condemned him to death. As recounted in Plato's *Crito*, he refused the opportunity to escape and live in exile.

Survey results

Surveys are highly suspect, particularly when they are conducted without the benefit of a historical perspective. Contributors to such surveys, moreover, often mistake charisma for leadership ability.

In the political domain, Arthur Schlesinger Jr.'s 1996 survey attempted to evaluate the quality of leadership exhibited by U.S. presidents on the basis of a single measure: performance in the White House.[4] Lincoln, Washington, and F.D.R. came in first, followed by Jefferson, Jackson, Polk, Theodore Roosevelt, Wilson, and Truman. (Some of the top nine, observed Schlesinger, made their mark without the benefit of a national crisis—Theodore Roosevelt, for one.)

Another survey taken by history scholars in 1997 produced dramatically different results.[5] (see Exhibit 10-2) Using a different (and imperfect) set of criteria (character, demeanor in office, fidelity to the Constitution, and contribution to the furtherance of human liberty), the survey understandably labeled two U.S. presidents as great: George Washington and Abraham Lincoln: Washington created the Continental Army, which won the American Revolution in 1783. He presided over the Constitutional Convention and ultimately served as the first president of the United States for eight years.

No one will argue with these selections.[6] It's hard to rationalize, however, the inclusion of Andrew Jackson, Dwight Eisenhower, and Ronald Reagan in the group of six near-great Presidents.

Jackson, despite a campaign as the leader of the "party

4 Arthur M. Schlesinger, Jr., opus citus.
5 Intercollegiate Studies Institute survey, National Review, October 27, 1997.
6 The survey conducted in 2002 by the Siena Research Institute ranked FDR, Lincoln, Theodore Roosevelt, Washington, and Jefferson as the greatest Presidents.
7 Thomas J. Neff and James M. Citrin, Lessons from the Top, Currency Doubleday, 2001.

of the people," did little for the working man and woman. He promoted the interests of slaveholders and abrogated a number of major treaties with the Native Americans. Eisenhower was a conservative whose greatest domestic achievement was to launch the Interstate Highway System, although he did end the Korean War and kept the peace afterwards. Reagan will be remembered best as the "great communicator." His advocacy of supply-side economics eventually generated massive federal deficits (he tripled the national debt), which produced high interest rates, an increase in the value of the dollar, and a reduction in the ability of U.S. industry to compete in world markets. He cut back on

10.2 | RANKINGS OF U.S. PRESIDENTS

Great	Low Average
George Washington	Martin Van Buren
Abraham Lincoln	Benjamin Harrison
	James Madison
	Rutherford B. Hayes
	George Bush
	Chester A. Arthur
	James Garfield
	Gerald R. Ford

Near Great	Below Average
Ronald Reagan	Woodrow Wilson
Thomas Jefferson	John F. Kennedy
Theodore Roosevelt	Herbert Hoover
Andrew Jackson	John Tyler
Franklin Roosevelt	Richard M. Nixon
Dwight D Eisenhower	Millard Fillmore

High Average	Failure
James Knox Polk	Franklin Pierce
Harry S. Truman	Ulysses S. Grant
John Adams	Warren G. Harding
Calvin Coolidge	Andrew Johnson
Grover Cleveland	Bill Clinton
James Monroe	Lyndon B. Johnson
John Quincy Adams	Jimmy Carter
William McKinley	James Buchanan
William Howard Taft	

affirmative action, and he relaxed safety and environmental standards. The Iran-Contra scandal came on his watch.

In a recent attempt to identify leaders in the corporate domain in the U.S., executive search consultants Thomas Neff and James Citrin combined the results of a Gallup poll with an analysis of corporate financial performance.⁷ They then reviewed the initial list of business leaders with colleagues to profile the "50 most successful." The research was comprehensive, and the ten criteria for defining success were plausible (financial performance, vision, ability to overcome challenge, customer focus, etc.) However, the results confirm the intrinsic fallacy of attempting to evaluate future impact by examining current behavior. Look at the nominees only two years after its publication. The strategic decisions by Armstrong (AT&T) and Koslowski (Tyco) have dramatically eroded shareholder value.[8] Trotman (Ford) must bear the responsibility for the Explorer tire fiasco. Lay (Enron) and Dunlap (Sunbeam) have been indicted for misleading shareholders. And so on . . .

If we venture outside of the U.S., it is just as easy to find examples of fall from grace. Percy Barnevik, chairman of ABB, was revered for his achievements. But after he retired in 1996, he received an undisclosed severance package of $87 million, and his opaque accounting practices deceived many investors. In retrospect, we see that Barnevik came close to wrecking the company.[9]

Using a similar polling approach for assessing corporate leadership, *Fortune* magazine proposes company reputation as a surrogate for a leader's ability to achieve and sustain high performance. Its annual survey of most-admired companies ranks them by eight attributes:

---

8 Koslowski's cupidity recently resulted in his indictment for evasion of New York State sales tax.
9 *Business Week*, March 25, 2002.

- Innovativeness
- Quality of management
- Employee talent
- Quality of products/services
- Long-term investment value
- Financial soundness
- Social responsibility
- Use of corporate assets

Executives who responded to the *Fortune* survey ranked quality of management and quality of products/services as the most important factors; they view financial measures as less important. Nevertheless, good leaders get high marks in each of the attributes.

The reputation of the ten top companies (listed in Exhibit 10-3) translates into higher market values than the laggards. But only a handful stays at the top of the rankings. Noteworthy are Northwestern Mutual Life in life insurance and Kimberly-Clark in forest products—both have led their industry sectors since the start of the surveys 19 years ago. And GE tops the overall list for the fourth year in a row. The other top firms rise and fall, however, with predictable frequency. Do they rise because of good leadership? Do they fall because leadership fails them?

Survey data simply do not help us answer these questions. At best, we can infer that surveys may tell us how well an organization is doing today. Evaluating effectiveness of leaders and organizations by a popularity poll is treacherous business. By the process of elimination, then, only one other metric remains—the legacy of the leader.

Legacy

If task completion, the leader's longevity, and his or her reputation are specious measures, we must consider the leader's legacy—the performance of the organization not only during his or her tenure, but after he or she are gone. (Some

10.3 | AMERICA'S MOST ADMIRED COMPANIES

1. General Electric
2. Southwest Airlines
3. Wal-Mart
4. Microsoft
5. Berkshire Hathaway
6. Home Depot
7. Johnson & Johnson
8. FedEx
9. Citigroup
10. Intel

Source: "America's Most Admired Companies", Fortune, March 4, 2002

egotistical leaders may want their successors to fail—it makes them look even better in hindsight!)

Great leaders have a global impact which is timeless. Good leaders may have only local short-term impact. The measure of a leader, in other words, depends both on the duration *and* the impact of his or her tenure. Ideas can have a life of their own. Organizations, however, can endure only if a leader develops a cadre of willing and able followers who can in turn become leaders. Writer and presidential advisor Walter Lippman captures one rationale:

The final test of a leader is that he leaves behind him the conviction and will to carry on. The genius of a good leader is to leave behind him a situation which common sense, without the grace of genius, can deal with successfully.[10]

10 Walter Lippman, "Roosevelt is Gone," *New York Herald Tribune*, April 14, 1945.

11 A recent analysis by Noshua Watson shows that "happy companies make happy

But this sets a low standard. Was the organization transformed? Did it continue to adapt and grow? Did the organization itself realize a long life? Did its behavior benefit the community? The legacy of the effective leader is an organization that, in the face of change and adversity, meets the unique needs of all its stakeholders—and hence endures. Most organizations fail this test, and, by implication, so do their leaders.

The metric itself is multidimensional. Increase in stock price, for example, does not capture the full impact of leadership on stakeholders other than the investors. These, then, are more appropriate criteria:

- Their organizations performed at a high level over a sustained period of time (GE and 3M)
- They did well for all stakeholders, not only shareholders, but employees, customers, and suppliers (Johnson & Johnson and Southwest Airlines)[11]
- They had significant impact on society as a whole (Microsoft and Intel)

The leader's scorecard will thus comprise these elements:

Stakeholder	Metric
Investor	Increase in shareholder value, achieved without chicanery
Employee	Loyalty and commitment to the vision
Customer	Quality of product or service and brand loyalty
Society	Benefit to the community and to mankind

investments." Stocks from the *Fortune* "best companies to work for" realized three times the annual return of the S&P 500 from 1998 to 2001. *Fortune*, May 27, 2002.

12 Although arguably Standard Oil survived first as Esso then as Exxon, and now as Exxon-Mobil.

In the business world, for example, corporations quickly come and go with predictable and depressing regularity; firms in every industry perish. Only 140 of the companies on the *Fortune-500* list in 1964 still retained their footing 30 years later. The others were either acquired by aggressive competitors, perished when they failed to adapt to new competitive threats, or saw the demand for their products and services decline. And take a look at the changing market value of firms in U.S. industry; not a single one of the top ten in 1917 endured to 2002 (Exhibit 10-4).[12]

10.4	SHIFTS IN MARKET VALUE			
	1917	**1967**	**1997**	**2002**
1	U.S. Steel	IBM	General Electric	General Electric
2	AT&T	AT&T	Coca-Cola	Microsoft
3	Standard Oil (NJ)	Kodak	Microsoft	Exxon Mobil
4	Bethlehem Steel	General Motors	Exxon	Wal-Mart
5	Armour & Co.	Standard Oil (NJ)	Intel	Pfizer
6	Swift & Co.	Texaco	Merck	Citigroup
7	Intl. Harvester	Sears Roebuck	Philip Morris	Intel
8	DuPont	General Electric	IBM	Johnson & Johnson
9	Midvale Steels	Polaroid	Procter & Gamble	AIG
10	U.S. Rubber	Gulf & Western	Wal-Mart	IBM

Source: "America's Most Admired Companies", Fortune, March 4, 2002

Authors of the flawed but immensely popular 1982 book *In Search of Excellence*, applied anecdotal evidence to develop a set of 43 top corporate performers.[13] During the ensuing

---

13 Thomas J. Peters and Robert H. Waterman, Jr., *In Search of Excellence*, Warner Books, 1982.

14 Arie de Geus, *The Living Company*, Harvard Business School Press, 1997.

20 years, however, many of them fell by the wayside. A few powerful companies, like IBM, Sears, and General Motors, stumbled badly but recovered with the help of new leadership. It seems that high performance, when it does materialize, does not persist. Technology firms are particularly vulnerable to extinction. Wang Laboratories and Computervision ranked as the largest computer software and service companies in 1980—today they're gone. Digital Equipment and Burroughs, major players in the computer-hardware industry, have been swallowed up by others. Netscape, creator of the original web browser, has been acquired and Exodus Communications, a major Internet-service firm, is in bankruptcy. Xerox is struggling to survive, and Polaroid is on the rocks.

Dutch-born economist Arie de Geus finds that seemingly invulnerable multinational corporations have an average life span of only 40 to 50 years.[14] There are some that qualify as long-term survivors, however. The Swedish firm Stora was established in 1288 as a mining company; it survives today as a diversified forest-products company.[15] Sumitomo, created in 1590 as a copper-mining enterprise, operates today as one of Japan's largest financial-services and trading companies.

Among other prototypes for longevity are DuPont, founded in 1802 as a manufacturer of gunpowder; it is now recognized as a major diversified manufacturer of chemical products, including nylon, Teflon, Lucite, Mylar, and Kevlar. Pilkington was established in England in 1826 as the St. Helens Glass Co; it is now one of the world's largest manufacturers of glass for building, automotive, and technical markets. Another glass company, Corning, got its start in 1851. The Procter & Gamble Company, producer of household products such as Tide, Ivory, Crest, Folgers, and Cover Girl, was formed in 1837. Several major insurance firms (MetLife, New York Life, Northwestern Mutual) got their start in the

15 Stora merged with Enso in 1998 to form the Stora Enso Corporation.
16 Richard Foster and Sarah Kaplan, *Creative Destruction*, Doubleday, 2001.

mid-19th century. Johnson & Johnson began in 1886 as a provider of antiseptic dressings for surgical and home use. Today it is a conglomerate that produces drugs, healthcare products, and medical supplies. William Boeing founded the Boeing Company in 1916; it is now the world's largest manufacturer of commercial airplanes and military aircraft. But these are all exceptions to the rule: most organizations die young.

The recent work of consultants Richard Foster and Sarah Kaplan further supports this conclusion.[16] They studied 1,000 companies in 15 major industries over the period from 1962 to 1998. None of the firms outperformed the average of its industry over the entire time. Only new emerging companies excelled—and only for a limited time. The authors argue that success handicaps established companies. Intent on serving their best customers, they overlook the threat from unfamiliar competition until too late. And the companies "built to last" pay the price in sub-par performance—the survivor's curse. Those who introduce new products and technology demonstrate better-than-average performance. Foster and Kaplan predict that in 25 years two-thirds of today's prominent corporations will have died or been acquired.

De Geus suggests that "companies die because their managers focus on the economic activity of producing goods and services, and they forget that their organization's true nature is that of a community of humans." This declaration recalls French philosopher Simone Weil's identification of *rootedness*—participation in the life of a community— as representing man's fundamental obligation to society.[17]

Why is longevity such an elusive goal—and why is corporate longevity decreasing so rapidly? According to de Geus, the four key contributors to corporate longevity are financial conservatism, cohesion (a strong sense of identity), tolerance for diversity within the organization, and sensitivity

17 Simone Weil, *The Need for Roots*, C.P. Putnam's Sons, 1952.
18 Some firms, like Suzuki and Exxon, have prospered despite their rigid

(adaptability to the environment). Stora, for example, shifted over the firm's 700-year history from copper mining to forestry to iron smelting to paper, wood pulp, and chemicals. Many are tempted to explain poor or erratic performance as the inevitable consequence of changes in technology, customer needs, competitor innovation, or the economy and other externalities. Complacency and a failure to keep an eye on the ball are cardinal sins in a world in which competitors show no mercy and the pace of change is rapid. This explains why so few firms succeed in moving outside of sectors in which they can utilize their core competencies. But even leaders who "stick to their knitting" can lose if they do not adapt to new challenges. Economic history teems with case studies of extinct firms who, like the mighty dinosaurs, failed to adapt, as we have demonstrated elsewhere. But good leaders anticipate changes and adapt to meet them—or better yet, initiate change and become dominant forces in their industry. They balance the creative tension between conservatism and adaptiveness

Few contemporary firms demonstrate this necessary quality.[18] GE stands out as one of the few exemplars of successful adaptation by diversification; it has prospered since its founding in 1892, and stands now as the only survivor of the original Dow Jones Industrial Average

What kind of leaders can beat the odds? Most followers today have little tolerance for autocratic leaders like Dunlap and Welch. Heroic leadership doesn't work anymore. This hypothesis is reinforced by consultant Jim Collins' recent research on "good to great."[19] From a data base of 1,435 companies, Collins selected those that had a record of sustained mediocrity followed by at least 15 years of outstanding performance, defined as outperforming the market by three to one. Only 11 survived the cut: Abbott

hierarchies, inflexible culture, and centralization, perhaps as the result of early investments in marketing and management.

19 Jim Collins, *Good to Great*, HarperCollins, 2001.

Labs, Circuit City, Fannie Mae, Gillette, Kimberly-Clark, Kroger, Nucor, Phillip Morris, Pitney-Bowes, Walgreen, and Wells Fargo. The cumulative returns of this group were 6.9 times the average of the general stock market—and all the qualifiers sustained their success under more than one CEO. However, Collins' list of stars may be no more reliable than the Peters and Waterman list of 1982. Gillette and Nucor are in trouble, and Wells Fargo has been acquired. And pacesetters like Cisco, GE, IBM, Intel, Amazon.com, and eBay fail to make Collins' roster of great companies. Yet his research does tell us one thing—companies can grow steadily if their leaders focus on the welfare of the institution rather than on short-term personal aggrandizement—they build companies that last.

Using this rationale, we arrive at a compelling argument for using legacy and historical perspective as the basis for assessing corporate leadership. Candidates for good leadership from the first half of the 20th century might include Henry Ford (founder of the Ford Motor Company), Andrew Carnegie and J.P. Morgan (founders of U.S. Steel), Alfred P. Sloan (President and CEO of General Motors), and Thomas J. Watson (architect of IBM's emergence as the computer-industry leader). Other examples of effective leaders include George Eastman (Eastman-Kodak), Estée Lauder (Estée Lauder) and Robert Noyce (Intel).[20]

My provisional choices from the past 50 years might include James Burke (former CEO of Johnson and Johnson, the diversified health-care company), Jan Carlson (former chairman of SAS, the Scandinavian airline), Michael Dell (founder of Dell Computer), William Gates (Chairman of Microsoft), Herb Kelleher (Chairman of Southwest Airlines), and Sam Walton (founder of Wal-Mart, the pioneering retail enterprise).

History has yet to deliver its verdict on many current leaders, including John Chambers at Cisco, Scott McNealy

---

20 Richard S. Tedlow, *Giants of Enterprise*, HarperCollins, 2001.

at Sun, Larry Ellison at Oracle, and others; the challenge is to distinguish between true leadership and the charisma that produces a cult of personality. A case in point is Jack Welch, former chairman of GE. Welch, who led GE from 1981-2001 was voted businessman of the year in 2001 in recognition of his success in running the company during a period of global competition and technological change. He was admired for increasing shareholder value, a popular current criterion for performance. However, in his relentless pursuit of this grail, Welch may have compromised GE's historic competencies in manufacturing and industrial production. (Whatever happened to GE's historic mantra "We bring good things to life"?) Welch transformed GE into a corporation that now derives more than 50 percent of its revenue and profit from financial services, and its ability to maintain its historic growth is dubious. Welch has also vigorously opposed EPA mandates to remove toxic PCB deposits from the upper Hudson River in New York State, residues from earlier GE manufacturing operations.

Ironically, the business world praised Welch's seven predecessors with equal enthusiasm during their tenure.[21] Charles Coffin saw GE safely through the great depression. Ralph Cordiner decentralized the corporation and began the diversification process. Reginald Jones, Welch's immediate predecessor, was designated the country's most influential businessman in 1979 and 1980. And so on. While none of these executives may have boosted shareholder value as much Jack Welch during their tenure, they laid the groundwork for GE's continuing evolution and prosperity.

What then is the agenda for effective leadership? The effective leader gives continuing attention to establishing values, purpose, and meaning, developing vision and direction, and building a supportive community. When one or more of these core elements is absent, the leadership is ineffectual and long-term performance suffers.

---

21 James Surowiecki, "Jack Welch, Average Guy," *The New Yorker*, December 18, 2000.

Leaders who lack values and purpose do not understand what's important, and their organizations become susceptible to tyranny, despotism, and a breakdown of the moral order. The leaders of such enterprises take them to the wrong place. Consider the regimes of Idi Amin of Uganda and Achmed Sukarno of Indonesia, or the leaders of the Columbia drug cartels. Or in the corporate world, similar examples include Al Dunlap of Sunbeam, John Rigas of cable giant Adelphia Communications, Bernard Ebbers of telecommunications giant WorldCom, and the Enron scoundrels Andrew Fastow, Jeff Skilling and Kenneth Lay.[22] Exhibit 10-5 describes this condition.

| 10.5 | LEADERSHIP WITHOUT VALUES AND PURPOSE |

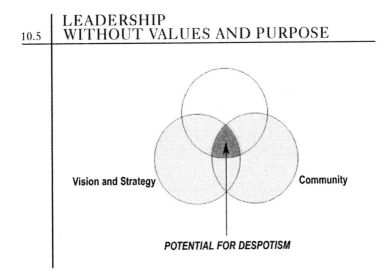

Leaders whose organizations have values, purpose, and vision, but no community fail to achieve their objectives. Inefficiency and conflict are common, and anarchy is one typical consequence. Leaders in such systems often turn to heroic measures, which can work for only a short time.

---

22 Rigas resigned after stockholders discovered that he had diverted substantial corporate monies to various private business ventures by members of his family. Ebbers, WorldCom's CEO, stepped down in 2002 after the company revealed that it had overstated its cash flow by $3.8 billion; he still owes the company $366 million for personal loans.

Consider the failed attempts of Indira Gandhi of India to reconcile the forces of global capitalism with the entrenched caste system and the legacy of Nehruvian socialism. Or Boris Yeltsin of Russia attempting to govern in a country seething with ethnic strife. In the corporate world, Citigroup is at risk. CEO Sandy Weill assembled a powerful group of financial-service entities—Travelers, Smith-Barney, Salomon Brothers—but their lack of a common culture puts them at risk. Exhibit 10-6 shows this situation.

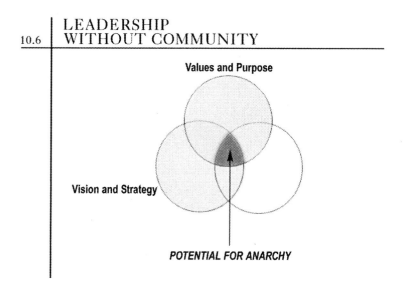

| 10.6 | LEADERSHIP WITHOUT COMMUNITY |

Leaders of organizations that have strong values and community—but no vision—don't know where to go. As a result, they go nowhere, stagnating in place or drifting along in a random walk. Many organizations in academia and the not-for-profit sector fit this model. And the Catholic Church is reeling today from the consequences of a failure to respect the changing needs of its members. Its refusal to acknowledge responsibility or complicity for the sexual abuses by its priests (in itself a grievous failure of values) has led to isolation from many of its constituents. Exhibit 10-7 portrays this problem. True leaders conjoin all the elements of leadership. They develop enterprises that combine moral purpose, vision, and strong community. If the leader has assembled the necessary resources to implement strategy, these enterprises have the potential for high performance, as illustrated in Exhibit 10-8.

10.7 | **LEADERSHIP WITHOUT VISION AND STRATEGY**

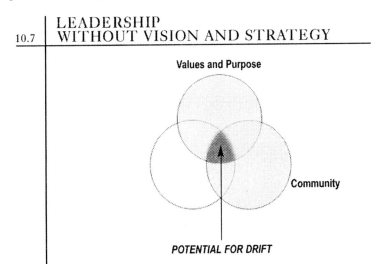

Values and Purpose

Community

POTENTIAL FOR DRIFT

10.8 | **FULLY-REALIZED LEADERSHIP**

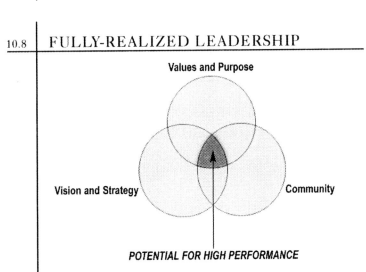

Values and Purpose

Vision and Strategy

Community

POTENTIAL FOR HIGH PERFORMANCE

A handful of companies are reaping the benefits of such enlightened leadership. On my honor roll are firms like 3M, Johnson & Johnson, Microsoft, Southwest Airlines, and Wal-Mart. Candidates for extinction include Xerox, Kodak, Hewlett-Packard and Compaq, and AT&T. To repeat the lessons of our analysis, then, we find that effective leaders realize high performance and longevity in their organizations by the way that they:

> Develop purpose and meaning; set direction and vision
> Inspire community to realize the vision
  o Support learning and adaptation; high diversity is a precursor to adaptation
  o Distribute the leadership role (imbed leadership in the fabric of the organization)
> Apply the right metric for performance

Will these axioms endure as we move into the 21st century? Let's take a look at some key trends.

Leadership challenges in the 21st century

Domestic, social, and economic forces seem to be overwhelming our leaders. Rapid change and chaos are the order of the day. New challenges continue to arise.

Rapid population growth will continue in Asia (especially in China; India, with laissez-faire family planning; and Pakistan, soon to be the world's third most populous nation) and Africa. The result is likely to be continuing human tragedy—50% of the world already operates below the starvation level.

In Europe and North America, on the other hand, we can expect significant declines in population. These will be unlike historic population reductions caused by war, famine, or plague. Fundamental social changes drive these trends: urbanization, global migration, changes in the role of women—

all have conspired to reduce total fertility rates (TFR) to less than the 2.1 children per family necessary to sustain

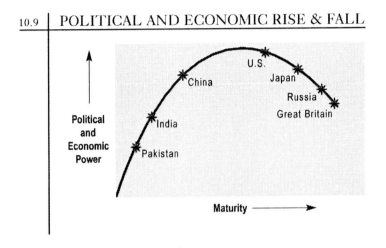

10.9 | POLITICAL AND ECONOMIC RISE & FALL

population.[23] As a result, in places like Italy and Japan, low TFR will produce population decline and an aging work force—these societies must cope with a smaller work force, reduced productivity, and a significant social burden for the government and for those who continue to work.

Literacy is increasing worldwide, driven by easy access to education via the Internet, although 70% of the world population cannot read today. Even in developed countries, distance learning will eventually become the dominant source of education.

The U.S. now reigns as the world's only superpower. But history shows that great empires have finite lives. China and eventually India will ultimately join and perhaps displace the U.S. as global superpowers. Western Europe is a potential force in world markets, but probably will not overcome centuries of conflict and mistrust among the countries that comprise the common market. (See Exhibit 10-9)

23 By the year 2015, 88 of the world's 180 countries will have replacement levels at or below the 2.1 threshold.

Resource shortages will begin to have global impact. The commodity in shortest supply will be water. The inevitable decline in fossil reserves will accelerate the development of alternative energy sources: wind, fuel cells, nuclear power, and fusion. Food technology will advance to meet growing needs: fish farming will replace animal farming; artificial food will find its way to the market.

Technology will continue to be a major driver of change. We can expect profound advances in nanotechnology, robotics, and optical computing. Applications of genomics will alter medical diagnostics and therapy: tissue engineering will produce designer plants, animals, and humans. Instant communications will give leaders access via the Internet to inexhaustible databases and a global forum for their ideas.

Despite the attempt to maintain trade barriers in some markets, globalization will increase. The gradual acceptance of the Euro in the common market in Europe is a portent of the trend. NAFTA will ultimately create a homogeneous North American market similar to the European Union. Parochial U.S. firms will find it necessary to compete in foreign markets, as their own domestic strongholds are invaded by foreign firms.

Social stresses will increase as a result of two important trends. The first is economic. Even in developing countries, the gap between rich and poor will get larger (50% of the world's population is already operating at or below the poverty level), creating severe social unrest. The second is religious. The religious schisms between Moslems, Hindus, Jews and Christians will continue. The conflict between the Israelis and the Palestinians seems unlikely to abate. New sects, like Mormonism (the fastest growing U.S. denomination with over 5 million members, plus another 6 million elsewhere) will gain power. We'll see little progress towards world peace, unfortunately.

The improvement in technology and communications is depriving leaders of their monopoly on information. Corporate leaders are losing control of their destinies (smarter customers, more agile competitors, increased complexity, greater uncertainty).

Followers have become more informed and educated, and they now know more than their leaders do. As a result, authority is devolving to the individual. Diversity will increase as more women and other minorities assume leadership roles. In the heroic era, leaders were lionized or canonized by Wall Street if their stock went up.[24] Now we will need to replace these false idols with leaders who are admired by the managers who work for them.

The corporation will become more and more dependent on virtual staff—free agents who have no permanent allegiance, but who operate in a flexible network. The consumer's demand for integrated products and services will force acceleration of strategic alliances among firms—the corporation that designs, builds, and distributes its own products will be an anachronism. This implies less competition and more collaboration. If we can be optimistic, our current system of global democratic capitalism can be replaced with coevolution.

Some final exhortations

How can leaders cope with what appears to be a monumental agenda for change? The reality is that every era has brought what appears to be an overwhelming list of leadership challenges.

To recapitulate, effective leaders adopt multiple roles, and they are effective primarily because of what they do. They clarify the values and purpose of their organizations. They develop inspiring visions and strategies. They build communities that share values, purpose, and mutual commitment. They get better at leading by developing their

---

24 In the brief period since stepping aside in 2001 as Chairman of GE, Jack Welch's reputation as a brilliant corporate leader has been badly tarnished. *The Economist*, once a staunch admirer of Welch's leadership, now excoriates him as an "aging philanderer" (May 4, 2002).

skill in initiating and managing change and by cultivating qualities of character, creativity, and compassion. And they guide the development of future leaders and, especially, of their successors.

In this post-heroic era, the leader's role is not merely to find a unique product or service that can satisfy the needs of a distinct market niche. Nor is it to maximize economic performance—as we've shown, a balanced scorecard for leaders and their organization entails a broader interpretation of the role of organizations and their members. Rather, good leaders develop organizations empowered to realize an enlightened purpose, move toward an inspiring vision, and value one another and their stakeholders. Leaders today must be catalysts for organizational self-renewal. And they must preach that the key to organizational longevity is the ability to develop a legacy that can rise above perturbation, variability, and uncertainty.

Exhibit 10-10 suggests an agenda for those who aspire to be effective leaders in this brave new world.

10.10 | THE AGENDA FOR THE LEADER

For the Organization

Reinforce values, purpose, and meaning

+ Establish a process to review and clarify the credo of the organization
+ Communicate the output to all stakeholders
+ Reward appropriate behavior

Create vision and strategy

+ Apply a scenario process to identify alternative futures
+ Create alternative visions and strategies and choose the best one to pursue
+ Assign responsibility and accountability for implementation

Build community

+ Create an adaptive culture, reinforced by rituals, symbols, and traditions
+ Design group experiences that promote interpersonal interaction
+ Enhance the qualities and skills of team with challenging projects
+ Treat stakeholders as ends, not means

For the Leader

Nurture the qualities of leadership

+ Sharpen self-awareness through contemplation balanced with experience
+ Develop character, keeping in mind the higher purpose
+ Cultivate creativity as the path to vision; experiment and take risks
+ Maintain commitment and a positive outlook

Acquire better skills

+ Learn to manage change and resolve conflict
+ Practice communicating by words and actions and listening with attention
+ Lead a life of balance and moderation
    + Mind
    + Body
    + Heart

Identify and develop those who will perpetuate a legacy

Appendix 10-A
The Allegory of the Cave

Socrates: Now let's think about the ignorance and education of human beings in the form of an allegory. Imagine human beings living underground in a kind of cave. The mouth of the cave, which is far above them, is as wide as the cave itself and opens to the light outside. These people have been here since childhood. Their legs and necks are chained so that they can't move. They can see only what is in front of them, because the chains are fastened in a way that keeps them from turning their heads. A fire burns at some distance above and behind them. If you look carefully, you can see a wall between the fire and the prisoners, like a curtain that hides puppeteers over which they show their puppets.

Glaucon: I can see that.

Socrates: Can you also see people passing behind the wall, carrying all kinds of objects above their heads so that they show over the wall? They are carrying statues of humans and animals made of wood, stone, and other materials. Some of them are talking and some of them are silent.

Glaucon: That's a strange image, and these are strange prisoners.

Socrates: They are like us. They see only shadows that the light from the fire throws on the wall of the cave in front of them—their own shadow of those of the objects passing behind the wall. Do you think they could actually see themselves?

Glaucon: How could they see anything but shadows if they are unable to move their heads?

Socrates: And what about the objects being carried by the people behind the wall?

Glaucon: They would see only the shadows.

Socrates: If the prisoners were able to talk with each other about these shadows, wouldn't they believe that they were discussing reality?

Glaucon: That's right.

Socrates: Suppose that the sounds coming from the people passing by echoed off the wall of the cave. Wouldn't the prisoners imagine that the voice they heard belonged to one of the shadows?

Glaucon: No doubt.

Socrates: So, it's obvious that for these prisoners the truth would be no more than the shadows of artificial objects.

Glaucon: That seems to be inevitable.

Socrates: Now let's consider the nature of their release and the cure for their ignorance. Imagine that one man is set free and forced to turn around and walk toward the light. Looking at the light will be painful; the glare will dazzle him and make it impossible to see the objects that previously appeared as shadows. Next imagine someone telling him that what he previously saw was an illusion, but that as he approaches reality it becomes visible. How would the prisoner respond? What if someone points to the objects as they pass and asks their names? Won't he experience great difficulty, considering the familiar shadows to be more real than the objects he sees now?

Glaucon: Much more real.

Socrates: And if the prisoner is forced to look at the light, won't that be painful to his eyes, causing him to take refuge in the shadows, which are easier to recognize than what is now shown to him?

Glaucon: That's true.

Socrates: Next imagine that he is dragged up the rough, steep path to the mouth of the cave and not released until he is in the presence of the sun itself. Don't you think that he would be pained and irritated at being treated this way? And when he is in full sunlight, won't he again be dazzled and unable to see any of the things that we would now say are real?

Glaucon: He wouldn't be able to see them right away.

Socrates: He would have to get used to seeing the world outside the cave. First he will recognize the shadows, then the reflections of other people and other objects in the water, and finally he could see the objects themselves. Then he will gaze at the night sky, better able to see the light of the moon and the stars than the sunlight or the sun itself.

Glaucon: That's probably how he would do it.

Socrates: At last he will be able to see the sun in its proper place, rather than its reflection in the water or somewhere else.

Glaucon: Now he would be able to do that.

Socrates: He would infer that the sun produces the seasons and the years, that is, rules over everything visible and is, in some way, the cause of everything that he and his fellow prisoners used to see.

Glaucon: Clearly that would be the natural path of his education.

Socrates: And when he remembers his old dwelling and what passes for wisdom in the cave among his companions, don't you think he would feel sorry for them and happy about the change that has taken place in himself?

Glaucon: There's no doubt about it.

Socrates: Let's suppose that the prisoners were in the habit of conferring honors and awards on those who are the quickest in seeing and remembering the appearance of the shadows, in saying which came first and which came later and which appear together. Do you think he would seek such honors or envy those who had won them? Wouldn't he say with

Homer that it's "better to be the poor servant of a poor master" and endure anything on earth than think as they do and exist in their condition?

Glaucon: Yes, I think he would put up with anything rather than lead that kind of life.

Socrates: Now imagine what would happen if he returned to his old place in the cave. If he suddenly came out of the sunlight, wouldn't his eyes be overcome by the dark?

Glaucon: At first he couldn't see a thing.

Socrates: It might take some time before his eyes adjusted, so if the prisoners were holding a contest and he had to compete with them in analyzing shadows while his eyesight was still weak, wouldn't he look foolish? People would say that he went up out of the cave and came back without his eyes, so there is not point in even thinking about making that trip. If someone were caught trying to release the prisoners and lead them up to the light, that person would probably be killed.

Glaucon: I'm sure you're right.

Socrates: Glaucon, my friend, you may now connect this allegory with what we were saying before. What we see with our eyes can be compared with the prison where people dwell, and the fire can be related to the power of the sun. You will not be far from my meaning if you consider the journey out of the cave and seeing the things there to be the ascent of the soul to the realm of what is knowable. This is my belief, which I have given at your request. It would take a god to know whether it is right or not. But regardless of whether it is true or false, I believe that in the realm of what is knowable the idea of the good appears last of all and can be seen only with great effort. Once we see it, we understand it to be the cause of all things that are right and beautiful, the source and ruler of light in this world and the ultimate source of truth and reason. This must be understood by anyone who wishes to act rationally and manage effectively either in public or private life.

Glaucon: I agree with what you say, as far as I can understand it.

Socrates: Then I would like your agreement on another matter. You shouldn't be surprised if the people who learn to think this way are unwilling to engage in everyday human affairs or—to continue with the symbolism from our allegory—if their souls naturally long for the realm outside the cave.

Glaucon: I agree that this would be quite natural.

Socrates: Nor should we be surprised if a person who passes from contemplating divine things to viewing miserable human affairs with blinking eyes should behave in a ridiculous way, especially if forced in law courts, or anywhere else, to dispute about the images of justice and meet the expectations of those who have never seen justice itself.

Glaucon: There's nothing surprising about that.

Socrates: Anyone with common sense will remember that the eyes can be confused in two different ways and from two different causes, either by coming out of the light or by going into the light. This is true of the mind's eye as well as the body's eye. If you remember this when you encounter someone whose vision is perplexed and weak, you will not be too quick to laugh. First you will ask whether the soul has come out of a brighter life and is unable to see because of the darkness or—having turned from darkness to daylight—is dazzled by the brightness. You would consider the one who comes from the light to be in a happy state of being, but you would pity the other one. And if you were inclined to laugh at either, it would be more reasonable to laugh at the one who comes from the cave into the light.

Glaucon: That's a good way to put it.

Socrates: But if this is true, those people are wrong who claim that they can educate by putting knowledge into an empty mind, like putting vision into a blind eye.

Glaucon: I have heard them make such claims.

Socrates: According to our account, the power is already in every soul. Just as the eye cannot turn from darkness to light without turning the whole body, when the mind's eye is turned around, the whole soul must turn from becoming to being and must be able to endure seeing its brightest form, which we call the good.

Glaucon: That is our account, and I think it is true.

Socrates: Perhaps there is an art that expedites this turning of the mind's eye, not by producing vision, which it already has, but by turning it in the right direction, which it lacks.

Glaucon: Yes, there must be such an art.

Socrates: The other so-called virtues of the soul are more like the qualities of the body. They are not innate, but are instilled by practice and exercise, whereas understanding comes from the gods and has an eternal power. But, depending on which way it is turned, it can either be useful and beneficial or useless and harmful. Surely you've noticed the cunning intelligence flashing from the keen eye of a clever villain and observed the passion with which a paltry soul finds the way to its goal. This kind of person is far from blind, but when keen eyesight serves evil, the greater the intelligence, the greater the crime.

Glaucon: I have often observed such people.

Socrates: Now consider sensual pleasures, such as those

that come from excessive eating and drinking, that naturally drag people down into the realm of shadows like lead weights. What if those weights were cut off in childhood? In that case they would be released from such impediments and turned in the opposite direction, so that the same soul in the same people would see the truth as keenly as it sees the shadows toward which it is now turned.

Glaucon: That would probably happen.

Socrates: Yes, and there is something else that is likely, possible even a necessary inference from what we have said. People without education and without experience of the truth will not be able to govern a republic, because they will lack the single purpose that could rule their private and public actions. There are others who never bring an end to their education; they will never act at all except under compulsion, imaging that they are already in the Islands of the Blessed.[25]

Glaucon: I think that's right.

Socrates: Then it is our responsibility as founders of the republic to compel the best minds to attain the knowledge we have called the greatest. They must climb to that height and arrive at the good. When they have done that and have seen enough, we must not allow them to do as they do now.

Glaucon: What do you mean?

Socrates: I mean that we must not allow them to remain in the realm outside the cave. They must be compelled to descend again among the prisoners in the cave and participate in their labors and their honors, whether these honors are worth having or not.

Source: Benjamin Jowett's translation, revised by Albert Anderson, Plato's Republic, Agora Publications, 2001.

25 In Greek mythology, the Islands of the Blessed are a kind of paradise in which good people dwell forever.

About the Author

Robert J. Allio has developed his perspectives on leadership over a long and successful career as an executive, educator, and management consultant. Since founding Allio Associates in 1979, he has worked with the leaders of many public and private organizations in the United States, Canada, Latin America, Europe, and Asia. His corporate history includes positions as president of Canstar, an early leader in the fiber optics industry, and senior executive roles with General Electric, Westinghouse, and Babcock & Wilcox.

He has served as chairman of a number of private firms, including Nicon and TracRac, managing director of the Anasazi venture firm, and a member of the board of TBS, GardenWay, Springboard, and Fourth Shift. His academic credentials include positions as Dean of the School of Management at Rensselaer and Professor of Management at Babson College.

Allio was the founding editor of *Planning Review* (now *Strategy & Leadership*) and was president of the North American Society of Corporate Planning. He has published extensively in the fields of strategy and leadership; his recent books include *The Practical Strategist* (Harper & Row) and *Leadership Myths and Realities* (Tata McGraw Hill).

He currently lives and works with his family in Providence, Rhode Island. Reach him at rallio@att.net.

Index